Living the Toughest Teachings of Jesus

RICK THOMPSON

▼ ● ◆ ■

VERNON GROUNDS

David C. Cook Publishing Co. Elgin, Illinois—Weston, Ontario

Living the Toughest Teachings of Jesus

© 1991 David C. Cook Publishing Co.

Published by David C. Cook Publishing Co.
850 North Grove Ave., Elgin, IL 60120
Cable address: DCCOOK
Designed by Randy Maid
Cover illustration by Guy Wolek
Inside illustrations by Bruce Van Patter
Printed in U.S.A.

ISBN: 1-55513-380-0

C ▾ O ◆ N • T • E ▾ N • T ◆ S

ARE YOU READY FOR A CHRISTIAN LIFESTYLE?

Ever noticed that you can swim along for years in the Christian life without leaving the shallow end of the pool? Then one day it hits you: If you're going to *do* anything about your faith, you've got to go deeper. If you're going to have a truly satisfying walk with God, you've got to plunge past surface spirituality, empty words, faith without action.

But you're wary. What will a really *Christian* lifestyle be like? Will you have to overcommit yourself? Will God demand the impossible of you? Will you have to erase your personality and become a musty, dusty saint from the pre-TV, pre-stereo, pre-microwave days?

Commitment for Today's Adults

Wary—that's how many of today's adults feel when they're urged to be "on fire for the Lord." They want to turn faith to action, but they've been raised to ask themselves, "What's in it for me?" They want to get serious about the Christian life—but in a new-fashioned way that works for them.

That's why we've introduced The Christian Lifestyle Series. It's designed to help today's adults "get real" about their commitment to Christ. Each course nudges them toward becoming more consistent disciples—without browbeating or boring them. Each session helps them to be honest about their struggles and take realistic, workable steps toward greater faithfulness.

Sessions for Today's Groups

Whether you lead a large Sunday school class or a small group, you know that today's adults hate five things:
- Boring lectures
- Lots of homework
- Being told what to think
- Subjects that have nothing to do with their everyday lives; and
- Courses that seem to go on forever.

The Christian Lifestyle Series lightens the load of lecture and increases active group participation. Each course offers reproducible student Resource sheets instead of requiring group members to read time-consuming, expensive student books. Each session asks for and respects group members' contributions and emphasizes real-life application. And instead of lasting twelve or thirteen weeks, each course wraps up in seven. If you want to fit a quarterly thirteen-week format, just combine two courses and skip the introductory session in one of them.

Format for Today's Leaders

Because you're busy, these sessions are easy to prepare and use. The step-by-step plans are easy to follow; instructions to the leader are in regular type, things you might say aloud are in bold type, and suggested answers are in parentheses.

A helpful article introduces the course, giving you an overview of the topic. The reproducible student Resource sheets are meant to be photocopied and handed out—or turn some into overhead projector transparencies if you like. Most sessions include a Resource sheet that will help prepare group members for your next meeting, too.

As always, feel free to adapt this course to the needs of your group. And may God use these sessions to help your group members discover the joy of a truly Christian lifestyle.

John Duckworth, Series Editor

THE TOUGH TEACHINGS OF JESUS

By Vernon C. Grounds

"**N**o one ever spoke the way this man does" (John 7:46). That was the admiring tribute of the temple guards who had been sent by the religious hierarchy to arrest Jesus, an assignment they failed to carry out.

That reaction to our Lord's teaching has been almost universal. People who heard Him in first-century Palestine, people who through the ages have read His words in the Gospels, people down to the present day—all have been tremendously impressed by what He said and the way He said it.

For example, English wit and author Malcolm Muggeridge makes this appraisal of the Sermon on the Mount: "No words ever uttered, it is safe to say, have had anything like the impact of these, first spoken to some scores, maybe hundreds, of poor and mostly illiterate people by a teacher that, in the eyes of the world, was of small account, at best another John the Baptist. . . . those words, those incomparable words were to echo and re-echo through the world for centuries to come . . . words that have gone on haunting us all, even though we ignore them; the most sublime words ever spoken."

What Makes Jesus' Teachings So Striking?

As we study the teaching of Jesus, what are some of its qualities that create the kind of reaction to which Muggeridge bears witness? What makes our Savior's words so arresting, so thought-provoking, so unforgettable even though they come to us in translation out of an ancient culture?

To be sure, Jesus unlike Paul did not attend a rabbinical school. Yet His probing insight and rhetorical genius compelled His listeners to exclaim, "How did this man get such learning without having studied?" (John 7:15).

Drawing on the rich resources of Semitic tradition and especially the Old Testament, Jesus used questions, aphorisms, antitheses, paradoxes, parables, and proverbs as He communicated His Father's truth to engrossed crowds or magnetized individuals. Endowed with a creative imagination, He, as was and still is common in the Middle East, had a vividly picturesque speech style, full of verbal pictures that imprinted themselves on the mind. But aside from these qualities, a cluster of characteristics stamped His teaching as strikingly unique.

For one thing, He spoke with authority (Matthew 7:29; Luke 4:36), a commanding conviction and persuasive power that compelled multitudes to listen. There was nothing tentative or indecisive about His discourses, His illuminating comments, and His stated beliefs. While not a bigoted dogmatist, Jesus could rightly be called dogmatic—a teacher who set forth His doctrine with an assurance that dissipated any semi-skeptical uncertainty.

For a second thing, He spoke with originality. Whether talking to one person or preaching to thousands, He taught with remarkable freshness, avoiding any appeal to the weary shibboleths and timeworn clichés of His rabbinic predecessors. Jesus not only issued a new theological currency; in effect, He also reminted the tarnished coin of truth.

For another thing, poetry marked His teaching, a diction with cadence, parallelisms, and metaphors that was like the Old Testament psalms and the soaring utterances of an Isaiah. Jesus did not deliberately versify, but His expression of spiritual realities was the opposite of flat prose. It was instead lucid, concise, linguistically rememberable—akin to, say, a hymn phrase like, "Were the whole realm of nature mine." That is why New Testament scholar C. F. Burney could write a whole book called The Poetry of Our Lord.

For still another thing, the teaching of Jesus was characterized by simplicity. It was totally free from technical terms and academic jargon. That explains why "The common people heard him gladly" (Mark 12:37, Amplified Version). Concrete, not abstract, His rhetoric was easily understandable, sparkling with graphic allusions to flowers, children, farming, sheep, bread, vineyards, fig trees, fishing, clouds, water, and countless other elements of everyday life. Commonplace objects and experiences became the means of illuminating the mysteries of the invisible world which sustains and pervades our physical world.

Yet at the same time the teaching of Jesus was marked by profundity. His fascinating parables, pithy epigrams, and enlightening flashes of humor revealed truth with shining clarity; but much of what He said had a depth of meaning that His hearers often did not realize. And some of His sayings, stories, and sermons were purposefully enigmatic, calculated to stimulate reflection and serve as a catalyst for reconsideration of long-cherished, superficial religious notions.

Hearers could no doubt shrug their shoulders if somewhat puzzled by the deliberately opaque elements in our Lord's rhetoric. But earnest truth seekers, their minds set in ferment by the master Teacher, were inspired to pursue the quest for a deeper knowledge of divine realities. And even though our Lord's words have been minutely analyzed by generation after generation of devout scholars, they remain tantalizingly inexhaustible.

The teaching of Jesus is also stamped by universality. It appeals to people on every level of culture in every country and every century. It intrigues the minds of philosophers, captivates the hearts of ordinary folk, and transformingly impacts lives everywhere. Jesus is thus what He audaciously claimed to be—the Light of the world.

Our Lord's teaching, to mention one additional quality, is marked by finality. Out of all the innumerable words spoken by human beings since the beginning of history, breathed out and forgotten, His have somehow survived. More than that, they continue to exert a powerful influence on men and women because they are an unimprovable source of insight concerning the ultimate issues of life, death, and eternity.

No matter, then, how immense our progress in all branches of learning and science may have been and will be, the teaching of Jesus can never become irrelevant or outmoded. His own prediction will be validated till the end of time: "Heaven and earth will pass away, but my words will never pass away" (Mark 13:31).

Studying the Tough Teachings

In reading and studying our Lord's teaching, some guidelines need to be followed.

1. The question, "What did Jesus say?" requires a further question: "What did He mean by what He said?"

This helps us avoid a wooden literalism. It's a reminder that we mustn't take figures of speech as informational statements or as obedience-demanding imperatives. When our Lord declares, "I am the door," He obviously doesn't want us to imagine that He is a piece of wood designed to close an opening. So when in Mark 9:43, 47 He talks about cutting off a hand or plucking out an eye, He isn't ordering self-mutilation. We must, therefore, use sanctified common sense and recognize that figures of speech are properly to be interpreted as figures of speech.

2. We mustn't be confused by our Lord's frequent recourse to exaggeration and hyperbole. What He does is simply a Semitic technique for giving forceful expression to an idea.

When a young lover assures his sweetheart, "I'd walk a million miles for one of your smiles," we don't accuse him of lying. We know that he's attempting to tell her how greatly she inspires and motivates him. In the same way Jesus resorts not to falsehood but to a faith-stretching figure of speech when He teaches His disciples in Matthew 17:20 that by the exercise of even minimal trust in God's power they can move mountains. Unless such an exaggeration is understood as Jesus intended it to be, we may accuse Him who is the truth of being a liar.

3. In studying our Lord's sayings, sermons, and stories, we must try to ascertain the basic principle or the one major directive He is communicating. We miss the real point if we engage in pointless efforts to squeeze significance from every word or phrase in His discourses and out of every detail in His parables. Take, for instance, the convicting tale which Jesus the master teller-of-tales told about the good Samaritan. This is the way it has actually been interpreted by some:

Man=Adam
Jerusalem=Paradise
Jericho=This world
Robbers=The devil and his angels
Wounds=Disobedience or sins
Priest=Law
Levite=Prophets
Good Samaritan=Christ
Beast=The body of Christ
Inn=Church
Two denarii=Two commandments of love
Innkeeper=Angels in charge of church
Return of the Good Samaritan=Second coming of Christ

In such allegorizing we lose sight of the parable's central lesson: Go and do as the good Samaritan did.

4. Analyzing Christ's teaching is not just an interesting mental game. It's an eternally serious business. Once we have grasped the meaning of His words, are we willing to face the challenge of the truth, believing Jesus, obeying Him, and making Him Lord of our lives?

DID HE REALLY SAY THAT?

Facing Up to Jesus' Radical Teachings

A friendly warning: These sessions are not entirely "safe"! They may raise more questions than your group can answer—and maybe some controversy, too. But that's the way it is with the toughest teachings of Jesus.

If you find you can't answer every question that arises during the course, don't worry. Encourage participants to keep looking for answers after the session, and to share their discoveries with the group. Keep encouraging your group to study the passages in an attitude of prayer, trusting the Holy Spirit to guide you into His truth.

Since it's easy to get bogged down on tangential issues when discussing these wide-ranging teachings, try to keep the group focused. But feel free to spend more time than allotted to important issues that your group needs to talk about.

If discussion catches on like wildfire, you could consider extending the course beyond seven weeks. You might even divide some sessions in half and spend two weeks on each, or spend whole meetings on the optional "Tough Stuff" steps described at the end of each session plan.

The aim of each session is to help group members—including yourself—decide what "next step" to take in applying these tough teachings. If you can accomplish that, you've done well indeed!

Where You're Headed:

To introduce the topic of the tough teachings of Jesus by discussing why Jesus said so many radical things; and to explore how we should approach His difficult words.

Scriptures You'll Apply:

Selected passages from Matthew, Mark, and Luke

Things You'll Need:

- Bibles
- Pencils
- Copies of "Did He or Didn't He?" (Resource 1)
- A variety of pictures of Jesus (optional)
- Copies of "Too Hot to Handle?" (Resource 2)
- Chalkboard and chalk or newsprint and markers (optional)
- Copies of Resource 3, "Be Prepared" (optional)

1
Breaking the Ice (optional)
(5-10 minutes)

Getting to Know Each Other

If the members of your group don't know each other very well, you might want to start the course with a fun getting-to-know-you activity.

Divide into teams with an equal number per team. (If your group contains fewer than ten members, do the following as one team.) When you say "Go," have every team member line up in alphabetical order of first names. See which team can accomplish this first. When teams are finished, have each person say his or her name slowly and loudly so that others are more likely to remember it.

Play other rounds if you have time, having teams line up in order of birthdays, length of time attending church, height, where born (nearest or farthest), etc.

2
Striking Statements
(5-10 minutes)

Starting to Think about the Many Tough Things Jesus Said

Give each group member a copy of "Did He or Didn't He?" (Resource 1). This sheet lists 25 statements. Have people work individually to cross off the ones they think Jesus *didn't* say. When most people are finished, go through these answers:

Jesus said #1 (Luke 9:60); #2 (Matthew 5:22); #4 (Mark 8:34); #5 (Matthew 7:6); #6 (Matthew 10:16); #7 (Matthew 10:34); #8 (Matthew 6:15); #9 (Matthew 15:24); #11 (Matthew 23:3); #12 (John 14:14); #13 (Matthew 23:24); #14 (Matthew 24:28); #16 (Matthew 6:24); #18 (Luke 12:49); #19 (Luke 21:25); #20 (Matthew 25:41); #21 (Matthew 5:29); #22 (Mark 10:11); #23 (Luke 14:26); #24 (Matthew 5:48); #25 (Matthew 10:5).

Jesus didn't say #3, #10, #15, or #17.

Any surprises on this list? (Let group members comment.)

3
Boy, This Is Hard!
(10-15 minutes)

Deciding Which of Jesus' Statements Are Toughest, and Why

Form smaller groups (four or five per group maximum). Give each small group about five minutes to go through the statements on Resource 1 and come up with the four or five its members consider the toughest. People should feel free to add other things Jesus said that aren't on this list.

Regather and have one person from each small group tell which statements were considered toughest and why. Then observe that in the weeks ahead you'll be studying #4, #8, #12, #16, #20, and #24. Chances are that some of these sayings were chosen as being among the toughest.

The difficult sayings of Jesus tend to fall into two categories:

1. Those that are difficult to understand—perhaps because of cultural differences, translation problems, or other reasons. Which sayings on Resource 1 would fall into this category? (Possibly #1, #5, #7, #9, #13, #18, #19, #25.)

2. Those that are all too easy to understand, but difficult to apply. What examples from the sheet can you name? (At least #4, #8, #16, #22.)

In a sense, these can be called the "radical" teachings of

Jesus. What do you think of when you hear the word "radical"? (One dictionary definition is, "Marked by a considerable departure from the usual or traditional; extreme.")

In this course we'll see over and over again how the words of Jesus stood in stark contrast to the conventions of His day—and our day. When this course refers to the toughest teachings of Jesus, it's these radical ones that we'll focus on.

You may want to share this quote from Mark Twain: **"The things in the Bible that bother me most are not what I don't understand, but what I *do* understand."**

4
Totally Radical

(20-25 minutes)

Discussing Why Jesus Said
So Many Radical Things

If possible, bring a variety of portraits of Jesus (cut from magazines, Sunday school material, etc.) and pass them around. Use these to get discussion about the "real" Jesus going, or just ask the following question:

What are some myths or misunderstandings about Jesus that are common today? (He was just a good man, a great teacher, just a baby in a manger, etc.)

How do the radical things Jesus said contradict some of these myths?

As needed, note that many people today prefer to view Jesus as a "safe" person who lived a good life and set a good example for us to follow. Many don't realize how radical He was—ruffling the Pharisees' feathers, upsetting the preconceived notions of his day, blasting apart hypocrisy, causing a stir wherever He went. He was anything but "safe." You may want to point out that many of the most common myths even can be found among Christians.

Why do you suppose Jesus said so many tough things? As needed, supplement answers with the following:

1. *To command attention.* Many of the things He said would cause people to sit up and take notice. He wanted to "upset the applecart."

2. *To force His hearers to think.* Much of what Jesus said had hidden, deeper meanings. If a hearer only took them at face value, he or she would miss what Jesus was really saying.

3. *To demonstrate His authority.* Only Jesus had the "right" to say many of the things He said. No one else could have said them. Jesus was speaking with all the authority of Almighty God Himself.

4. *To make a point and make it stick.* Not only did Jesus get His message across—He did it in ways that would easily be remembered.

You might even say that the difficult things Jesus said are a "proof" that He lived and taught on earth. If the Gospel authors had made up His teachings, they wouldn't have included so many hard-to-follow commands. Swiss scholar P. W. Schmiedel, in the *Encyclopedia Biblica*, said that so many of the sayings of Jesus conflict with the image of Him that quickly became conventional in the Church that "it is ludicrous to think that the early Church invented them."

But what should we do with the difficult teachings of Jesus?

How should we approach them?

Allow for replies. Then distribute copies of Resource 2, "Too Hot to Handle?" Go over the suggestions as a group. See whether group members can add suggestions to the list.

5
Where to from Here?

(10 minutes)

Previewing the Coming Weeks' Topics

Preview the course ahead with comments like these, adapted to fit your situation:

In the weeks ahead, we'll be looking at six tough teachings. Each session uses a focus statement of Jesus to introduce the topic and then explores many other verses on the same topic—usually concentrating on what Jesus had to say about it.

Statement 1: "Deny yourself, take up your cross, and follow me." The theme is total commitment. What does it cost to follow Jesus?

Statement 2: "If you do not forgive men their sins, your Father will not forgive your sins." This session will be on the challenge of forgiveness. Will God forgive me if I don't forgive others?

Statement 3: "Ask me for anything in my name and I will do it." That's high-powered faith. Can we really move mountains?

Statement 4: "You cannot serve both God and Money." Why can't we have our cake and eat it, too?

Statement 5: "Depart from me, you who are cursed, into the eternal fire prepared for the devil and his angels." Fire and brimstone—would a loving God really send someone to hell?

Statement 6: "Be perfect, therefore, as your heavenly father is perfect." Perfectly holy. Why did Jesus tell us to be perfect? What did He mean?

See if there are any questions about where you are heading. Which topics are people most looking forward to and why? Which do you expect to be most controversial?

If you want group members to read some of next week's Scripture verses in advance (which can save considerable group time), pass out copies of Resource 3, "Be Prepared."

If you aren't using the optional Step 6, close in prayer. Ask for God's guidance in the weeks ahead.

6
Tough Stuff (optional)

(5-10 minutes)

Exploring the Stickier Issues

If your group wants to go further, wrestling with some of the more difficult or controversial questions raised by Jesus' teachings, try the "Tough Stuff" option at the end of each session. You may need extra time to tackle these thought provokers; consider adding a week or two to the course for "Tough Stuff" if your group likes the challenge.

Choose questions that you think will help you meet the objectives you've established for your group.

What do you suppose each of the following groups would think of the tough teachings of Jesus?

What teachings might they embrace or reject?

Which groups would have the hardest time accepting His

teachings, and why?

Which would have the easiest time?

The list of groups:

Corporate executives
Practicing homosexuals
Political leaders
Those involved in cults
"Sunday" Christians
People in this church
Single parents
Adult children of alcoholics
Homeless people
Someone on death row
Drug addicts
Drug pushers
College professors

In what ways is your own concept of Jesus too safe?

You might want to have group members interview acquaintances with the question, "Who is Jesus?" or "What is Jesus like?" Have interviewers report findings to the rest of the group at the start of next week's session.

DID HE OR DIDN'T HE?

Look over each of the following statements and cross off all those that you think Jesus *didn't* say.

1. Let the dead bury their own dead.
2. Anyone who says, "You fool!" will be in danger of the fire of hell.
3. Accept me as your personal Lord and Savior and you shall inherit eternal life.
4. If anyone would come after me, he must deny himself, take up his cross and follow me.
5. Do not give dogs what is sacred; do not throw your pearls to pigs.
6. Be as shrewd as snakes and as innocent as doves.
7. I did not come to bring peace, but a sword.
8. If you do not forgive men their sins, your Father will not forgive your sins.
9. I was sent only to the lost sheep of Israel.
10. The Lord helps those who help themselves.
11. They do not practice what they preach.
12. Ask me for anything in my name and I will do it.
13. You strain out a gnat but swallow a camel.
14. Wherever there is a carcass, there the vultures will gather.
15. Follow me and I will prosper thee.
16. You cannot serve both God and money.
17. Anyone who calls me "Lord, Lord" will enter the kingdom of heaven.
18. I have come to bring fire on earth, and how I wish it were already kindled!
19. There will be signs in the sun, moon, and stars.
20. Depart from me, you who are cursed into the eternal fire prepared for the devil and his angels.
21. If your right eye causes you to sin, pluck it out.
22. Whoever divorces his wife and marries another, commits adultery against her.
23. If anyone comes to me and does not hate his father and mother . . . he cannot be my disciple.
24. Be perfect.
25. Go nowhere among the Gentiles.

TOO HOT TO HANDLE?

What should we do with the toughest teachings of Jesus? How should we approach them?

1. With prayer and the guidance of the Holy Spirit.

2. By reading the account in more than one Gospel (if recorded there). Often the wording will be slightly different and shed new light on the subject.

3. By looking at the context (events immediately before and after) of what Jesus is teaching. Who is He talking to? At what point in His ministry is He saying this?

4. By interpreting His teachings in light of everything else He said. Avoid basing a doctrine on one verse or passage in isolation. If we did that, we could build a case for some pretty odd teachings. One example: Jesus' words in Luke 14:26, where He tells His disciples to "hate" their parents and siblings. What He may be saying is that our love for Him must be so great that our love for our own families pales in comparison. Taken out of context, this teaching could lead to some dangerous application.

5. By laying aside your preconceptions and misperceptions about Jesus. Don't try to keep Jesus in a box that you've created. Let Him expand your view of who He is.

6. By consulting trustworthy commentaries, but realizing that even they might be wrong. Attempts have been made, even by well-meaning people, to "explain away" some of Jesus' more difficult sayings ("That teaching only applied to His culture," "He was only speaking figuratively," etc.).

7. By reading the difficult passage in more than one translation.

8. By admitting that the sayings are hard and seeking to find application in your own life. What is the next step you should be taking as a result of this teaching? The next step, even if it is a small one, is the most important step. It is only when we acknowledge that these are radical sayings that we can find ways to apply their truths to our own lives.

"It will simplify the discussion if we admit the truth at the outset: that the teaching of Jesus is difficult and unacceptable because it runs counter to those elements in human nature which the twentieth century has in common with the first—such things as laziness, greed, the love of pleasure, the instinct to hit back and the like. The teaching as a whole shows that Jesus was well aware of this and recognized that here and nowhere else lay the obstacle that had to be surmounted."

(T. W. Manson, *The Sayings of Jesus.*)

BE PREPARED

To prepare for the next session, please read Mark 8:31–9:1. Then jot down your responses to the following.

Observe _____

(include the verses before and after the passage)

Who is this spoken to?

Where does this take place?

When does this take place?

Key words:

Contrasts:

Interpret _____

What is Jesus saying? (put it in your own words)

Why do you suppose Jesus said this?

List any questions this passage raises in your mind:

Apply _____

What is this passage saying to you personally?

What are you going to do about it?

For "extra credit": Read

Matthew 16:24-28; Luke 9:23-27.

TOTAL COMMITMENT
Taking Up Your Cross

"If anyone would come after me, he must deny himself and take up his cross and follow me" (Mark 8:34b).

On the surface, this tough teaching of Jesus may seem pretty straightforward. But it's one of the most difficult for people today to put into practice.

"When Christ calls a man, he bids him come and die." So wrote Dietrich Bonhoeffer in *The Cost of Discipleship*. Christ's call to deny ourselves, take up our cross, and follow Him goes against the grain of human nature. We'd rather indulge ourselves, take it easy, and follow our own desires. This is a hard saying of Jesus—not so much in the sense that it's hard to understand, but in that it's hard to follow.

Since it would be impossible to examine all the implications of these radical words in one (or a dozen) sessions, you'll want to help group members focus on specific steps—no matter how small—that they can begin taking this week in response to Christ's command.

Where You're Headed:
To help group members begin to understand what it means in their daily lives to deny self, take up their crosses, and follow Jesus.

Scriptures You'll Apply:
Mark 8:31—9:1; Matthew 16:24-28; Luke 9:23-27; and other passages

Things You'll Need:
• Copies of "The First EZ Church" (Resource 4) and one or more actors to read it (optional)
• Pencils or pens
• Bibles
• Copies of "Three Giant Steps" (Resource 5)
• Chalkboard and chalk, newsprint and markers, or overhead projector
• Copies of Resource 6, "The Challenge of Forgiveness" (optional)

1
Ad-dressing the Issues

(10-15 minutes)

Demonstrating "Easy Believism"

As people arrive, have them work in groups of three or four to create radio commercials for a make-believe church that goes out of its way to make it "easy to be a follower of Jesus." The point is to humorously contrast what it really means to follow Jesus with what some people today wish it would mean.

Give groups five to ten minutes to develop their commercials. Encourage them to use humor and creativity. When ads are finished, gather as a large group and share your creations.

If you're short on time, or if you'd rather not have groups create ads, simply have one or more volunteers read aloud the commercial on Resource 4, "The First EZ Church."

After sharing a good laugh, move the discussion to more serious matters with questions like the following.

What element of truth did you find in this/these advertisement(s)? (We sometimes try to cheapen God's grace by sugarcoating the commands of Christ.)

Is it easy to be a disciple of Jesus, or difficult? (It's both. It's easy to receive salvation, and Christ says His yoke is easy and His burden is light. Yet it's difficult to truly be obedient, to follow His commands daily.)

Dietrich Bonhoeffer wrote that cheap grace is "grace that we bestow upon ourselves." What are some examples of how people today try to "cheapen" God's grace or make it easy? (Some examples: Forgiveness without repentance; membership without church discipline; communion without confession; making Christianity only an intellectual faith without need of contrition; not living any differently from the way rest of the world lives.)

Today we're going to look at one of Christ's toughest teachings: "If anyone would come after me, he must deny himself and take up his cross and follow me" (Mark 8:34b). These words stand in stark contrast to those of the world, and even those of some churches today.

What did Jesus mean when He said this? Are people who claim to be His followers really following as He directed? Let's look into that.

2
He Was Kidding, Right?

(10-15 minutes)

Comparing the Words of Jesus in Three Gospel Accounts

Write the following references on chalkboard, newsprint, or overhead projector: Matthew 16:24-28; Mark 8:34—9:1; Luke 9:23-27. Then direct: **Read all three passages. Use your Bible to note context (setting, timing, etc.) of each. Then write down major similarities and differences among the three passages.**

Let group members work individually or in small groups. After about ten minutes, discuss results.

What did you learn from this exercise? Let people volunteer answers, supplementing with the following as needed.

Differences:

Mostly, the differences between these three accounts of the same event are minor. This lends credibility to the fact that Jesus really said this. The differences reflect each author's emphasis.

Here are some of the things that are unique to each:

Matthew 16:24-28—reward each person according to what he's done (vs. 27); doesn't have the line about being ashamed; uses Son of Man (vs. 28).

Mark 8:34—9:1—calls disciples and the crowd (vs. 34); and for the Gospel (vs. 35); adulterous and sinful generation (vs. 38); come with power (9:1)

Luke 9:23-27—take up cross *daily* (vs. 23), which makes the teaching more specific; forfeit his very self (instead of soul) (vs. 25); doesn't have the line about "or what can a man give in exchange for his soul."

Similarities

The passages are more similar than they are different. Here are three key similarities:

Context. In all three Gospel accounts, this teaching comes immediately after Peter's confession of Jesus as the Christ. This is definitely the turning point in each Gospel. Also, the Transfiguration is the next recorded event in all three accounts. This has led some to believe that the line about "some who are standing here who will not taste death before they see the kingdom of God come with power" refers to the Transfiguration. Three other interpretations are commonly offered—the destruction of the temple in 70 A.D. (Christ coming in judgment); the resurrection and Ascension of Jesus; or Pentecost (the Holy Spirit coming to establish the Church). This final view is the most commonly accepted.

Teaching. All three emphasize these major points: If you would come after Me (Jesus) you must deny self, take up cross and follow; paradox of saving and losing life; what good is it to gain the whole world and forfeit your soul/self; Christ is going to come in the glory of the Father and of His angels; some standing here won't taste death before seeing the kingdom come in power.

Initiative. Jesus takes the initiative to gather people to hear this teaching in all three accounts.

What do you suppose prompted Jesus to give this particular teaching at this particular time? (Peter just proclaimed Him Messiah, then rebuked Him for saying He would suffer. Jesus seems to be saying that all true followers are called to a similar fate. Perhaps Peter's protest sprang from his own unwillingness to suffer.)

What's so radical about these words? (They are contrary to human nature—self-denial, taking up a cross, losing life rather than saving it, etc. This passage presents a clear choice between two extremes. There are no other options. It's either salvation in Christ, or forfeiting one's soul. People want to try to gain the world *and* salvation, but Christ teaches that it's one or the other.)

Is it possible to be a "nominal" Christian? (This is a very difficult question, because many churches are full of people who might be classified as "nominal" Christians. Jesus, however, didn't seem to leave any room for such a category. John Stott, in his book, *Basic Christianity* [InterVarsity Press, 1958] has this to say about nominal Christians: "People still ignore Christ's warning and undertake to follow him without first pausing to reflect on the cost of doing so. The result is the great scandal of Christendom today, so-called 'nominal' Christianity. In countries to which Christian civilization has spread, large numbers of people have covered themselves with a decent, but thin, veneer of Christianity. They have allowed themselves to become somewhat involved; enough to be respectable but not enough to be uncomfortable. Their religion is a great, soft cushion. It protects them from the hard unpleasantness of life, while changing its place and shape to suit their convenience. No wonder the cynics speak of hypocrites in the church and dismiss religion as escapism." You might want to read this quote to your group and let them respond to it. So, the best answer to the above question is for each of us to examine our own relationship with Jesus and see if we are following Him fully. Understanding what He expects from us is a good place to begin this examination.)

We're now going to take a closer look at the three basic commands of Mark 8:34—denying self, taking up our cross, and following Jesus to see what's really involved at each step.

3
Easier Said Than Done
(15-20 minutes)

Taking a Closer Look
at the Three Giant Steps
of Mark 8:34

Give everyone a copy of "Three Giant Steps" (Resource 5). As a large group or in three smaller groups, work through the verses and questions. Save the "personal application" sections for later in the session. Share results.

As needed, use the following information to supplement and stimulate discussion. Some of the comments are based in part on the books, *The Hard Sayings of Jesus* by F. F. Bruce (InterVarsity Press) and *The Cost of Discipleship* by Dietrich Bonhoeffer (Macmillan).

1. Deny yourself

What it means: Jesus is calling us to "die to self." It's more than skipping dessert for Lent, or refusing to buy something until it goes on sale. It's a continual saying no to one's self-centered will for the sake of Christ. It involves the willingness to let go of our own selfish ambitions and accomplishments. It's a choice we need to keep on making every day. The same verb is used of Peter's denial of Christ; we are to disown ourselves as totally as Peter disowned Jesus. Denying self is to be so totally aware of Christ that we put His needs and wishes above our own. Paul provides an excellent example of self-denial in the Philippians 3 passage.

What the world says: Indulge yourself; put yourself first; treat yourself; it may cost more, but I'm worth it; go ahead, you deserve it; look out for #1, etc.

Why is it so hard to deny ourselves?

Is it really possible to be oblivious to your own needs and desires in order to follow Christ? Is that what this passage is teaching?

Does this teaching conflict with the Bible's other teaching to love ourselves? (Not really; it's possible to love someone and deny him or her something. For example, a parent might deny a child candy before supper.)

Is it possible to take self-denial too far? If so, give some examples.

Does Christ want us to give these things up, or merely be willing to give them up?

2. Take up your cross

What it means: It's more than what we usually mean when we say, "It's the cross I must bear" (having noisy neighbors, in-laws, nearsightedness, etc.). It means we are to "carry the death of Christ with us," to "share in His sufferings." It was not an uncommon sight in Jesus' day to see people carrying their crosses as Jesus did to a public execution. Carrying the cross involves suffering, rejection, and shame, even death itself for the sake of Christ. There is a positive side to suffering for Christ; not only can it bring about personal growth, but it allows us to share in His glory. Suffering is not an accident, but a necessity.

What the world says: Take it easy; be cool; avoid pain; take the path of least resistance; take care of yourself, etc.

Should a Christian seek out opportunities to suffer?

If a Christian isn't suffering, is there something wrong?

How can we tell what our "cross" is?

3. Follow Me

What it means: It's a daily decision to follow Jesus, not just a one-time commitment. It's a *complete submission* to His will—on His terms, not our own. It involves *death to self* and *obedience* to His commands. As Bonhoeffer puts it, "only he who believes is obedient, and only he who is obedient believes." The disciples demonstrated their faith (though imperfect) by their act of following Jesus. Following Jesus also involves *insecurity*—if there were no insecurity, there would be no opportunity for faith. Following Jesus involves *leaving*—leaving without looking back. To the disciples it meant leaving their old ways behind and following Him to death and eternal life. Finally, following Jesus involves *service*—we follow Him in order to serve Him.

What the world says: Follow your hunches; follow your star; follow your hopes and dreams; be true to yourself; do your own thing; follow the crowd; to each his own, etc.

What are the costs and benefits of following Jesus?

What's the alternative?

Where are some places we might be asked to follow that we would rather not go?

Wrap up this step with comments like these:

Jesus presents us with a choice: "If anyone would come after me . . . " He doesn't force us to follow Him.

These three steps are connected. Only when we are willing to deny ourselves can we take up our cross and follow Him. If we're putting our own needs first, we won't be able to do it. Sometimes, the suffering that results from self-denial is part of carrying the cross.

Note that Jesus' first words to Peter (Mark 1:17) and His last words to Peter (John 21:22) were to follow Him. These are obviously important words.

4
Driving It Home
(10 minutes)

Choosing Principles from
This Session to Apply

Give people a few minutes to fill out the "personal application" sections of Resource 5. You might help them respond, using questions like the following.

Deny yourself: In other words, what things are most likely to keep you from truly following Jesus? What might hold you back? What might you be tempted to rely upon instead of Him?

Take up your cross: If people have difficulty with this question, ask what is the hardest thing they have to bear at this time in their lives. Is it a relationship, a personality characteristic, a life circumstance? How might that involve suffering for Jesus?

Follow Me: Emphasize the words "specific" and "this week." What is one thing people will do differently this week as a result of today's session?

Then have people pair off and share one or two answers to the questions. Let individuals decide how much they are willing to share. Encourage group members to take the sheet home and give it more thought this week.

At the end of your time together, have pairs pray for one another—for the Lord to help them keep their commitments and to really know what it means to follow Him this week.

If you want students to prepare for your next session, give everyone a copy of Resource 6, "The Challenge of Forgiveness."

5
Tough Stuff (optional)
(5-10 minutes)

Exploring the Stickier Issues

If the church today took these words more seriously and really counted the cost of following Jesus, how might things be different?

Would there be more or fewer followers?

How might church business meetings be different?

Do you think allocation of church funds would change?

Read some or all of the following case studies aloud. After each case, ask: **In light of Christ's call to deny self and take up the cross, how would you respond to each of these people?**

Susan—**She "went forward" during the altar call at church when she was younger. It was an intensely emotional experience. She felt truly sorry for her sins, asked forgiveness, and felt very close to God. Today she considers herself a born-again Christian, but is living a sexually permissive lifestyle. She stays away from the church because she feels the people there judge her.**

Frank—**He's a well-meaning older gentleman. Some would say he's a pillar of the church and community. He considers himself a very committed Christian and has some very strong opinions about eternal security, the inerrancy of the Bible, and other matters. Though he wouldn't admit it, he's also prejudiced against African-Americans and has no mercy for those on welfare.**

Cheryl—**She's very active in social concerns—working to feed the hungry and shelter the homeless. She's very turned off by "born-again" Christians and doesn't want to be associated** with them. She's never "gone forward" or "prayed the sinner's prayer" but she feels she is doing what Jesus wants her to be doing.

Jeff—An active leader in a fellowship group during college, he was instrumental in leading several people to the Lord and discipling them. Today he's living in total rebellion—he wants nothing to do with God or the church.

After discussing the cases, acknowledge that there are no easy answers to these situations. It's important to realize that all people, including ourselves, are sinners and stand in need of God's grace. We can help others look at the words of Jesus and challenge them to come to grips with His words. But the first step each of us can take is to examine our own behavior in the light of this tough teaching of Jesus.

THE FIRST EZ CHURCH

Are you tired of going to a church that demands something of you in return? Are you fed up with being asked to volunteer your time—or worse yet, give up some of your hard-earned money? Then you should check out the First EZ Church—if you want to, that is.

We've done everything we can to make your visit enjoyable. We've . . .
• Replaced those hard, wooden pews with overstuffed recliners;
• Eliminated disgusting words like "sin," "guilt," and "service" from our vocabulary; and
• Added valet parking.

Then there's our patented "Select-a-Song" music system. Just put on the headset, punch in the name of your favorite kind of music, and sit back and enjoy the sweet, sweet sounds. Choices include pipe organ, orchestra, synthesizer, heavy metal, and accordion—to name a few.

We would never require you to sing along. But if you choose to, we've rewritten some of the timeless hymns to bring them up to date. Here are just a few of the favorites we offer:

> • **"Take My Wife, and Let Me Be"**
> • **"Banking on the Promises"**
> • **"A Mighty Mattress on My Bed"**
> • **"Joyful, Joyful, I Adore Me"**
> • **"Blest Be the Tie That Blends with My Suit,"** and the ever-popular
> • **"Great Is My Faithfulness."**

All our services last less than half an hour. We've cut out the boring sermon, endless Scripture readings, and long-winded prayers. And if it's too much bother to make one of our eleven services, simply order a copy on videotape and worship in the privacy of your home anytime you choose.

So, if it's not too much of a hardship, please worship with us at the First EZ Church, located at 100 Bliss Road—across from the convenience mart.

THREE GIANT STEPS

Deny yourself

Luke 14:25, 26
John 12:23-25
I Corinthians 15:31-34
Philippians 3:7-10

What It Means

What the World Says

Personal Application
What would be the hardest thing(s) for me to give up in each
of the following areas?

    Relationships

    Personal ambitions

Take up your cross

Matthew 27:27-44
Luke 14:27-35
Romans 8:17, 18
II Corinthians 4:10, 11

What It Means

What the World Says

Personal Application
What are some specific ways in which I probably will suffer as
a result of following Jesus?

Follow Me

Matthew 4:18-22
Matthew 19:27-30
Luke 9:57-62
John 12:26

What It Means

What the World Says

Personal Application
What are some specific things I can do to follow Jesus more closely this week?

The Challenge of Forgiveness

To prepare for next time, please read Matthew 6:9-15.

Observe

(include verses before and after the passage)

Who is this spoken to?

Where does this take place?

When does this take place?

Key words:

Contrasts:

Interpret

What is Jesus saying? Put it in your own words.

Why do you suppose Jesus said this?

List any questions this passage raises in your mind:

Apply

What is this passage saying to you personally?

What are you going to do about it?

For "extra credit": Read
Matthew 5:21-24; Mark 11:25; Luke 6:37; Matthew 18:21-35; Luke 17:3, 4; John 20:19-23; Luke 23:34.

THE CHALLENGE OF FORGIVENESS

June 6 93

If We Won't Forgive, Will He Forget?

"If you do not forgive men their sins, your Father will not forgive your sins" (Matthew 6:15).

Jesus knew how difficult it was for people of His day to forgive each other. He knew that anger, jealousy, bitterness, resentment, hate, seeking revenge, and holding grudges were some of the side effects of harboring an unforgiving spirit. Not much has changed in 2,000 years!

Jesus had some pretty strong things to say about forgiveness—words that are just as relevant today as when He first spoke them. The focus of today's session will be on forgiving one another—not on God's forgiveness of us, though a celebration of God's forgiveness is included. We can more fully appreciate God's forgiveness when we have been forgiven by another, or have forgiven someone else.

If you can get only one point across in this session, stress that the responsibility for forgiveness is in our own court—whether we've wronged someone or been wronged by someone. It's up to each of us to take the necessary steps toward reconciliation.

Where You're Headed:

To take a fresh look at Jesus' words on forgiveness in order to examine our own relationships and see where action on our part is needed.

Scriptures You'll Apply:

Matthew 6:9-15; other Gospel passages

Things You'll Need:

- Copies of "What Would You Do?" (Resource 7)
- Pencils or pens
- Bibles
- Copies of "Forgive or Forgo" (Resource 8)
- Chalkboard and chalk or newsprint and markers (optional)
- Copies of Resource 9, "High-Powered Faith" (optional)

1
Case in Point

(10-15 minutes)

Discussing Case Studies
on Forgiveness

Give everyone a copy of Resource 7, "What Would You Do?" People can read the three case studies individually or in small groups and write their answers to the questions on the handout.

When most people appear to be finished, have a few volunteers share their answers. Don't spend too much time on any one case; use the cases to introduce the topic of forgiveness, stressing how difficult it can be to ask for and give it.

If you have extra time, try acting out each situation. Assign people these parts:

Situation 1: You and the soloist the next time you have an opportunity to talk.

Situation 2: You and the neighbor later that morning.

Situation 3: You and the parents of the teen at church a while later.

Which is harder, to ask for forgiveness, or to forgive someone? (Answers will vary depending on the situation and the temperaments of the individuals involved.)

Is it ever impossible to forgive another person for something? (In our own strength, yes—but with God's help, no.) Ask for examples of forgiveness that must have been very hard for individuals to give, that must have been made possible by the Lord's power.

What are the consequences of failing to forgive someone when we have a grudge against him or her? (Stress, bitterness, etc.) See whether anyone quotes Matthew 6:15, the focus of this session. If no one mentions the verse, read it yourself.

Do most Christians act as though they take this verse seriously?

What if the person in the wrong shows no repentance?

What if you've wronged someone, and the person refuses to accept your apology?

Don't attempt to answer these questions now. Simply raise them and tell group members that you're going to look at what Jesus had to say about forgiveness—in order to develop principles for being more forgiving people.

What examples of forgiveness can you think of from Jesus' life? (Forgiving His executioners from the cross; restoring Malchus's ear; forgiving Peter for denying Him, etc.)

2
Against the Grain

(15-20 minutes)

Understanding Forgiveness
from Gospel Passages

Give everyone a copy of "Forgive or Forgo" (Resource 8). Have people fill out the first section. You could assign teams to answer questions A and B for each set of verses, or complete them as a group.

Here are some guidelines to aid your discussion:
Matthew 5:21-24; Mark 11:25

A. *About God*—These verses show that God cares more about us being in a right relationship with others than about our offerings and prayers.

B. *About forgiveness*—It's our responsibility to take the initiative to heal the relationship if we have wronged someone (Matthew 5), or have been wronged by someone (Mark 11). Taking steps toward reconciliation is in our court.

Matthew 6:9-15; Luke 6:37

A. *About God*—He's in heaven. He's holy. He gives us things. He has the power and ability to forgive us. It's His will that we forgive others.

B. *About forgiveness*—It must be an important issue to Jesus, because it's the thing He comments about after sharing His model prayer. It's the concept from the prayer He chose to expound on. In His model prayer, Jesus seems to assume we will forgive ("as we forgive our debtors"). Note: Some commentators have explained that Matthew 6:15 is talking about personal fellowship with God, not salvation from sin. In other words, God's forgiveness is not based on ours; but our forgiveness of others is based on our realizing that God has forgiven us.

Matthew 18:21-35; Luke 17:3-4

A. *About God*—He's like a king who has some tremendous debtors. He's gracious and just.

B. *About forgiveness*—It has to be "from your heart," or sincere. The unmerciful servant jeopardized his own forgiveness by failing to forgive his debtor. It's important to note that the unmerciful servant owed the king "millions of dollars" yet was owed "only a few dollars." The contrast is intended to be striking. There's no limit to how often we should forgive someone. The Matthew passage does not imply that the debtor has repented; the Luke passage does. It seems that our responsibility is to forgive whether forgiveness is asked for or not.

John 20:19-23; Luke 23:34

A. *About God*—He set the ultimate example of forgiveness on the Cross. Forgiveness was obviously important to Jesus, because He taught about it after the Resurrection in the John passage.

B. *About forgiveness*—It's costly. The John passage may seem to imply that we have some degree of control over whether other people are forgiven. But as the *NIV Study Bible* text notes explain, John 20:23 is literally, "'Those whose sins you forgive have already been forgiven; those whose sins you do not forgive have not been forgiven.' God does not forgive people's sins because we do so, nor does he withhold forgiveness because we do. Rather, those who proclaim the gospel are in effect forgiving or not forgiving sins, depending on whether the hearers accept or reject Jesus Christ."

Move on to Part II of Resource 8. Give people a few moments to fill in some responses to questions A through E. Here are a few thoughts to guide your discussion:

A. *What does it mean to "forgive"?* The dictionary lists these three definitions:

• Cease to feel resentment against an offender; pardon

• Give up a claim to something (perhaps bitterness, revenge, getting even)

• Grant relief from payment; excuse

We see all three of these definitions in various Scripture verses.

B. *Who are we to forgive?* Anyone who is a debtor.

C. *When are we to forgive?* Whenever we are wronged, and especially before worship.

D. *Why are we to forgive?* Because God cares about whole relationships.

E. *How do we forgive?* From the heart. It has to be authentic, not just lip service. By canceling someone's "debt."

To wrap up this step, you may want to read this quote from author Lewis Smedes: **"To forgive is to put down your 50-pound pack after a 10-mile climb up a mountain. . . . To forgive is to set a prisoner free and discover the prisoner was you. To forgive is to reach back into your hurting past and recreate it in your memory so that you can begin again. . . . To forgive is to dance to the beat of God's forgiving heart. It is to ride the tide of love's strongest wave. Our only escape from history's cruel unfairness, our only passage to the future's creative possibilities, is the miracle of forgiving."** (From "Forgiveness, the Power to Change the Past," *Christianity Today*, January 7, 1983.)

3
Your Move
(15-20 minutes)

Applying Principles of Forgiveness to Our Own Relationships

Form groups of three or four. Read aloud each of the following statements, pausing to let members of each group complete the statement for each other if they're comfortable doing so. If possible, spouses shouldn't be in the same small group.

• **Sometimes it's hard for me to forgive because . . .**
• **A person or group I've needed to ask forgiveness of . . .**
• **A person or group I've needed to forgive . . .**

Then ask:

What might be involved in forgiving each of the following? Have small groups discuss their responses to these situations:

• Mrs. A wronged you years ago, and probably doesn't think about it anymore. It still bugs you, but bringing the situation up might be opening old wounds.

• Mr. B hurt you deeply, but has come to ask your forgiveness.

• Mr. B hurts you again, and begs your forgiveness again.

• Ms. C continues to hurt you and shows no sign of remorse or repentance.

Have volunteers share the results of their discussion. As needed, supplement with the following thoughts.

• *Mrs. A*—It might be best to simply let go of your grudge, and not bring it up with her.

• *Mr. B, first offense*—Your forgiveness could be demonstrated by a hug, a note, or some other visible act.

• *Mr. B, second offense, and Ms. C*—In cases like these it may be very difficult to forgive someone. Forgiveness might mean letting go of our bitterness or resentment; giving up any plans to retaliate; not taking sadistic satisfaction in the person suffering or being punished; not gossiping about the person; not ignoring the person in social gatherings; confronting or rebuking the person in an attitude of love. With Ms. C, you might need to take action to get the person to see his or her sin.

If you take only one thing home from today's session, remember this: Whether you have been wronged, or wronged

someone else, the ball's in your court to take the first steps toward reconciliation.

4
Forgiving Fest

(5 minutes)

Celebrating God's Forgiveness

Our focus today has been on our need to forgive one another. Our understanding of the importance of forgiving others grows deeper when we think about how much God has forgiven us. Let's spend a few minutes in prayer, focusing on God's forgiveness.

If you have time, you might lead group members into prayer by reading Scriptures about forgiveness (such as Psalm 103:8-13; I John 1:9, 10; Micah 7:18, 19; Ephesians 4:32.)

After prayer, ask:

How does your experience of God's forgiveness affect your own ability to forgive or ask for someone's forgiveness?

If you wish to prepare people for the next session, distribute Resource 9, "High-Powered Faith." Encourage group members to look up the verses and answer the questions this week.

5
Tough Stuff (optional)

(5-10 minutes)

Exploring the Stickier Issues

What if a Christian died while harboring an unforgiving spirit against someone else? Would it make a difference in God's forgiveness? In God's reward?

God is always willing and ready to forgive us, but He waits for us to repent. Should we wait for repentance before offering someone forgiveness? It might be good to read Matthew 18:15-17. If the person who wrongs you shows no repentance, then you are to treat him or her like a pagan or a tax collector. Keep in mind how Jesus treated pagans and tax collectors—He ate with them and loved them!

What situation would be the hardest for you to forgive someone for? (Someone who murders a family member, sexual abuse, etc.) **Suppose you found yourself in this situation. What shape would your forgiveness take?**

Must we always feel forgiveness, or is showing it sufficient?

Is it possible to forgive and forget? Or is that something only God does?

Once we've forgiven someone, should we act as if nothing ever happened? Or does the relationship have to change?

WHAT WOULD YOU DO?

Read each of the following cases and imagine that it happened to you. Answer the three questions following each situation.

Situation 1

It's after church and you're talking with a friend about the service. You make a joke about the soloist who sang off-key—something about wishing you had brought a pair of ear-plugs. You get a sinking feeling when you notice your friend's face—the soloist is right behind you, and probably heard everything you said! You discreetly slip out of the church, but you feel terrible.

What action do you need to take?

Why might that be hard to do?

What actions would you be tempted to take instead?

Situation 2

It's 5:00 A.M. and you are rudely awakened by the neighbor's dog—for the third time this week. You get up and look out your window and see that the dog is in your yard, tearing up your flower garden—for the third time this week. Your neighbor seems oblivious to the whole thing. You try going back to sleep, but you can't—for the third time this week!

What action do you need to take?

Why might that be hard to do?

What actions would you be tempted to take instead?

Situation 3

One of your best friends is killed in a car accident, hit by a drunk driver. Some high school kid had too much to drink at a graduation party and was driving in the wrong lane. You feel sick when you find out that the party where the alcohol was served was at the home of some people who go to your church. Apparently the parents knew about and allowed the drinking. You're not sure what to do with your feelings.

What action do you need to take?

Why might that be hard to do?

What actions would you be tempted to take instead?

FORGIVE OR FORGO

PART 1

Read each set of verses and answer these two questions:

A. What do these verses say about God and/or Jesus?
B. What do these verses say about forgiveness?

Matthew 5:21-24; Mark 11:25
A. About God:

B. About forgiveness:

Matthew 6:9-15; Luke 6:37
A. About God:

B. About forgiveness:

Matthew 18:21-35; Luke 17:3, 4
A. About God:

B. About forgiveness:

John 20:19-23; Luke 23:34
A. About God:

B. About forgiveness:

PART 2

A. What does it mean to "forgive"?

B. Who are we to forgive?

C. When are we to forgive?

D. Why are we to forgive?

E. How do we forgive?

HIGH-POWERED FAITH

To get ready for the next session, please read John 14:12-14.

Observe *(include verses before and after the passage)*

Who is this spoken to?

Where does this take place?

When does this take place?

Key words:

Contrasts:

Interpret

What is Jesus saying? (put it in your own words)

Why do you suppose Jesus said this?

List any questions this passage raises in your mind:

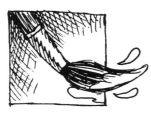

Apply

What is this passage saying to you personally?

What are you going to do about it?

For "extra credit": Read
Matthew 6:30; 8:26; 14:31; 16:8; 17:20; Mark 16:14;
Matthew 8:10; Luke 8:48; Matthew 9:29; 15:28;
Luke 7:50; 17:19.

HIGH-POWERED FAITH
Can We Really Ask Him for Anything?

"**Y**ou may ask me for anything in my name, and I will do it" (John 14:14).

These words can be frustrating. Not everything we pray for happens the way we want it to—even some good, worthwhile things. It's important to look at what Jesus meant by faith and what He expects from us. This session seeks to do just that.

Most of Jesus' teaching about faith was in the "laboratory of life." He used events as they happened to teach about faith. The focus of this session will be these life events. We'll look at six passages in which Jesus said, "You of little faith," and six passages in which Jesus attributes great faith to individuals. These events hold some clues as to what faith is and isn't.

In order to take a fresh look at faith, we need to confront some of the misunderstandings people have about it. Jesus makes it quite clear that we only need faith the size of a mustard seed in order to move mountains; He'll do the rest. But what is mustard seed-sized faith? How can we help group members (and ourselves) have the type of faith Jesus is talking about? As you lead this session, may you and your group gain new insight into being people of faith.

Where You're Headed:
To contrast good and bad examples of faith from the Gospel accounts so that group members can come to a greater understanding of what it means to have faith in the Lord.

Scriptures You'll Apply:
John 14:12-14; selected Synoptic Gospel passages

Things You'll Need:
• Copies of "About Faith" (Resource 10)
• Pencils or pens
• Pieces of scratch paper (optional)
• Bibles
• Copies of "Haves and Have Nots" (Resource 11)
• Chalkboard and chalk, newsprint and markers, or overhead projector
• Copies of Resource 12, "It's Only Money" (optional)

Faith Is . . . 1

(10-15 minutes)

Defining Faith and
Discussing Common
Myths about It

As group members arrive, give each person a copy of "About Faith" (Resource 10). People should work individually on this. Encourage them to be creative. After a few minutes, ask for a few volunteers to explain their drawings of faith. Then have several read their definitions of faith.

What do our definitions and drawings have in common? Make a list of the common elements in the drawings and definitions. Your list might include words like believe, trust, being sure of things hoped for and not seen (Hebrews 11:1).

You may want to quote *The New Bible Dictionary* (InterVarsity Press, 1962): **"Faith is the attitude whereby a [person] abandons all reliance on his own efforts to obtain salvation, be they deeds of piety, of ethical goodness, or anything else." Also, faith is "the attitude of complete trust in Christ, of reliance on him alone for all that salvation means." Faith involves an intellectual assent (belief), an emotional assent (trust), and a response (obedience).**

What are some common misconceptions about faith that people have today? Make a list of these as well. People can start the discussion by sharing some of the things they listed under "Faith isn't" on Resource 10. Some common myths might include:

• We need to have great faith (actually we need only have a little faith in a very big God).

• Having faith is a way to get whatever we want out of God.

• Faith is something other people have; it's only for super-saints, not ordinary people.

• All sickness and pain are results of lacking faith.

• We should never doubt.

• Faith is purely passive.

Describe the condition of your faith in three words or less.

Ask for volunteers to share what they wrote, but don't force anyone to do so. If people seem reluctant to talk, you might want to have everyone write down a number from 1 to 10 on a piece of scratch paper; 1 means "not at all satisfied with my level of faith," and 10 means "completely satisfied with my level of faith." Collect the papers and read the responses.

Faith is a word we hear all the time in the church. But what is it really? Do we really experience the kind of faith Jesus talks about? Today we're going to take a look at faith, mustard seeds, and moving mountains.

He Said . . . 2

(15-20 minutes)

Looking at Faith in
the Gospel of John

The word "faith" is found only twice in the Old Testament. It occurs over 240 times in the New Testament. Today we'll be focusing on what Jesus had to say about it.

Jesus uses the noun "faith" only once in the Book of John in the *New International Version*. He uses it a lot more in the other three Gospels. But he uses the verb "believe" much more in John than in the other Gospels.

Have someone read John 14:12-14.

What's so radical about these words? (We should expec. doing greater things than Jesus did. That's pretty mind-boggli. We can ask for anything in Jesus' name and He will do it.)

Do you think most Christians today live as if they really believe this? Why or why not?

What does "in my name" mean? Note that this must be an important concept because it's used in verses 13 and 14. Commentaries agree that it is certainly more than tacking the words "in Jesus' name" to the ends of our prayers. To pray in His name means in accord with His nature, His will, His work on earth. God will grant those requests that further His purposes.

Why does our doing greater things than Jesus depend upon Jesus going to the Father (vs. 12)? (Because it's only after Jesus goes to the Father that He is able to send the Holy Spirit to us. And it's only by the Holy Spirit's power that we are able to do greater things. See John 14:16, 17 and 15:26.)

What was Jesus' motivation to do whatever we ask in His name? (To bring glory to the Father—verse 13.)

How do these verses enhance or enlarge your concept of faith, if at all?

After listening to replies, move on to the next step. Or, if you have ample time, you might want to explore a similar teaching in Matthew 21:21, 22 and Mark 11:20-25 about the withered fig tree and moving mountains.

3
A Study in Contrasts
(15-20 minutes)

Discovering People Who Did and Didn't Demonstrate Faith

Give everyone a copy of "Haves and Have Nots" (Resource 11). Form at least two groups. One group should look at the six accounts of the Have Nots—those who demonstrated a lack of faith—and fill in the two columns for each passage. They will need to read more than the verse listed to get a feel for what's going on in each passage. The other group should do the same thing for the verses listed under "Haves."

If one group finishes before the other, encourage those who are done to write down any lessons about faith that their verses teach them. Then bring the whole group back together and share results.

As needed, supplement with the following information:

Have Nots

Who was Jesus talking to? The disciples. In the Matthew 6 passage, it's the disciples and a crowd (the Sermon on the Mount—see Matthew 5:1). Is it possible that Jesus had higher standards for His disciples? These men left everything to follow Him. They had many lessons to learn, but when they received the Holy Spirit they demonstrated great faith.

What did He rebuke them for?

Matthew 6:30—Worrying about what to wear; worrying about inconsequential things.

Matthew 8:26—Being afraid of the storm, even after Jesus has demonstrated His power in other ways.

Matthew 14:31—Doubting. Peter actually took a step of faith when he climbed out of the boat. But when he took his eyes off Jesus, he began to doubt.

Matthew 16:8—Not learning a lesson. Not understanding. The disciples still didn't see "the big picture."

Matthew 17:20—No power due to lack of faith. Apparently the disciples tried without success to heal the boy. The statement about the mustard seed and moving mountains is certainly worth exploring. What do your group members suppose Jesus meant by this? Why do you suppose Jesus used such strong words in Matthew 17:17?

Mark 16:14—Lack of faith and stubborn refusal to believe the reports of those who had seen the risen Lord. Note the verses that immediately follow Jesus' rebuke; He speaks about the powerful things His followers will do if they really believe in His name.

Haves

Who was Jesus talking to? To those who would have been considered by the Jews to be foreigners or outcasts—A Roman soldier, a Canaanite woman, a Samaritan leper, a woman who suffered chronic bleeding, blind men, and a sinful woman. Perhaps Jesus was making a point by choosing these people as His examples of faith. Our faith isn't dependent upon who we are, our standing, or works, but on who He is.

What did they do that showed faith?

Matthew 8:10—Sought Jesus out and asked for help; believed in Him; believed that He could heal, even from a distance.

Luke 8:48—Sought Jesus out; touched His cloak; admitted her actions.

Matthew 9:29—Followed Him; called out to Him; believed He could heal them.

Matthew 15:28—Sought Him out; called out to Him; was persistent; was willing to settle for "crumbs."

Luke 7:50—Came to Jesus; visibly demonstrated her love by wiping His feet with her tears. She "loved much." Note that Jesus forgave her sins based on her active love. Then He rewarded her for her faith. Through faith she was saved, and her faith was shown by her actions.

Luke 17:19—Met Jesus where He was; called out to Him; obeyed Him by going to the priest; worshiped Him; gave thanks to Him. The leper's faith made him well, but his faith was demonstrated in action.

What lessons about faith do these verses teach you? (Some suggestions: We need to seek Jesus out and trust in Him, not in our own power. We should bring our worries, doubts, and fears to him instead of trying to keep them hidden. We should keep our eyes on Him, not be stubborn, demonstrate our faith through specific acts, and not wait to act until we feel we have enough faith.)

4
Faith Meets Life

(5 minutes)

Listing Personal Faith
Obstacles and Faith Builders

Recap the content from the Bible passages by making two lists on a chalkboard, newsprint, or overhead projector. Label one list "Obstacles" and the other "Faith-builders." Under "Obstacles," list things that can keep us from having more faith. Under "Faith-builders," list things that strengthen one's faith. Have group members call out items that should be on each list. Your lists might look something like this:

Obstacles
Worrying about things
Fear of things beyond our control
Unresolved doubt/continuing unbelief
Not understanding/not learning a lesson
Not relying on the Holy Spirit's power
Stubbornness

Faith-builders
Seeking Jesus out/calling on Him
Asking for help/bringing our problems to Him
Being humble
Following Him
Believing His words/believing in His name
Being persistent
Performing specific acts of love
Obedience
Worshiping/thanking Him

When your lists are complete, challenge everyone to choose one item from each list to focus on in the coming week. People might want to write their responses on the back of one of their handouts. Share commitments as appropriate, one-on-one, in small groups, or all together.

What new insights into faith, if any, have you gained from today's session?

After listening to replies, close in prayer (unless you plan to use Step 5). Ask God to help your group members have the kind of faith Jesus described, in order to bring glory to Him.

If you want to prepare people for next time, hand out copies of Resource 12, "It's Only Money." Encourage group members to look up the verses and answer the questions before the next session.

5
Tough Stuff (optional)

(5-10 minutes)

Exploring the Stickier Issues

There are no easy answers to the following situations and questions. But your group may find discussing them a profitable challenge. As you discuss, remind group members that the crucial thing is to recognize our responsibility to cleave to Jesus, trust Him, and not try to use Him as a vehicle to get our own wishes.

Discuss each of the following scenarios in light of Jesus' teaching about faith:

a. A young man is dying of cancer. A well-meaning friend tells him that it is God's will to heal him, and that he should have faith that he will be healed. The young man's friend quotes Mark 11:24: "Therefore I tell you, whatever you ask for in prayer, believe that you have received it, and it will be yours."

b. A devout Christian woman prayed daily for forty years for the salvation of her husband. He died, apparently an unbeliever.

c. A man prayed earnestly to be delivered from a habitual sin. He confessed his sin to the elders of his church. During a prayer service, the elders laid hands on him and anointed him with oil. For a while he felt delivered. But now he's beginning to slip back into his old ways.

d. A woman feels tremendous guilt because her mother died of a terminal illness. She had been praying for her mother's healing. When her mother's condition began to worsen, the daughter began to doubt that God would heal her mom. Soon after, her mother died.

It's clear that God doesn't answer all prayers in the affirmative. Jesus' request not to "drink the cup" in the Garden of Gethsemane, and Paul's request to be delivered of his "thorn in the flesh" are two examples. How do you reconcile this fact with Jesus' claim that anything we ask for in prayer will be granted to us?

Can Christians literally move mountains, or was Jesus speaking symbolically? If He was speaking symbolically, what did He really mean? What would be an example of moving a mountain?

Draw "faith":

What faith is:

What faith isn't:

Describe the condition of your own faith in three words or less:

HAVES AND HAVE NOTS

Jesus taught many lessons on faith in the "laboratory of life." Look up and read each verse. Then look at the context of that verse; what's going on around it? What's the situation? Then answer the two questions for each verse. When you're finished, summarize what you've learned by answering the question at the bottom of the page. If there's still time, write on the back of the sheet any questions you have about faith.

Have Nots

	Who was Jesus talking to?	What did He rebuke them for?
Matthew 6:30		
Matthew 8:26		
Matthew 14:31		
Matthew 16:8		
Matthew 17:20		
Mark 16:14		

Haves

	Who was Jesus talking to?	What did they do that showed faith?
Matthew 8:10		
Luke 8:48		
Matthew 9:29		
Matthew 15:28		
Luke 7:50		
Luke 17:19		

What lessons about faith can be learned from these verses?

IT'S ONLY MONEY

To prepare for next time, please read Matthew 6:19-24.

Observe

(include verses before and after the passage)

Who is this spoken to?

Where does this take place?

When does this take place?

Key words:

Contrasts:

Interpret

What is Jesus saying? *(put it in your own words)*

Why do you suppose Jesus said this?

List any questions this passage raises in your mind:

Apply

What is this passage saying to you personally?

What are you going to do about it?

For "extra credit": Read
Matthew 6:1-4; 17:24-27; 19:16-26; 22:15-22; 23:16-24;
Mark 12:41-44; 14:1-9; Luke 6:24, 25, 30; 10:33-35;
12:13-21, 31-34

IT'S ONLY MONEY
You Can't Have It All, After All

"**Y**ou cannot serve both God and Money" (Matthew 6:24).

Though they probably wouldn't admit it, many people wish the above verse weren't in the Bible. Of all the sessions in this course, this one is likely to generate the most controversy. Nowhere are the commands of Jesus more out of line with current thinking and practice than in the area of money. Nowhere do His commands hit closer to home—right in our own wallets.

As you prepare this session, keep in mind that your goal is to help each group member take that "next step" toward greater faithfulness, whatever it may be. For some this may mean being more responsible with a credit card; for others, canceling the purchase of a luxury; for still others, giving sacrificially to the poor. Your job is to help group members look again at the words of Jesus on this subject, then trust the Holy Spirit to convict each person about putting the commands into practice.

Because of the controversial nature of Christ's words on the subject, you may find some commentators trying to explain away or lessen the severity of what He is saying. It may help to keep in mind that if we were really taking care of each other's needs as the Lord intended, His sayings about money might make more sense to us today.

Fasten your seat belt. The ride might be a little bumpy. But if this session helps your group take a new look at Jesus' teachings on money, it'll be worth the ride.

Where You're Headed:
To develop a set of principles about money in order to come closer to living the way Jesus intends for us to live.

Scriptures You'll Apply:
Matthew 6:19-24 and other synoptic Gospel passages about money

Things You'll Need:
- Copies of "For the Love of Money" (Resource 13)
- Pencils or pens
- Small prize (optional)
- Bibles
- Copies of "On the Money" (Resource 14)
- Chalkboard and chalk or newsprint and markers
- Copies of Resource 15, "Fire and Brimstone" (optional)

1
Money Business

(5-10 minutes)

Taking a Silly Test to
Introduce a Very
Serious Subject

Give everyone a copy of Resource 13, "For the Love of Money," and about five minutes to complete it. When most are finished, share the following answers. Encourage group members to keep track of their own points.

1. Let people judge their own answers. Have those who were very close (or way off the mark) show their drawings.
2. b. (18 months)
3. c. (8.6 billion)
4. d. (Dire Straits)
5. c. (1 ton)
6. d. (None of the above. Paul said, "For the love of money is a root of all kinds of evil" in I Timothy 6:10.)
7. 1=k
   2=g
   3=h
   4=e
   5=f
   6=d
   7=c
   8=i
   9=b
  10=j
  11=a
  12=l

8. Let group members be the judges here. A couple of possibilities: *The Money Pit* and *The Color of Money*.

Scoring: 1 or 2 points for question 1, 1 point for a correct answer to questions 2-6. 1 point for each part of question 7 (12 points total), 1 point for question 8. Total possible points: 20.

Have participants share their scores. You might want to award a small prize to the person(s) with the *lowest* score, for showing so little concern about money.

2
Dollars and Sense

(5-10 minutes)

Discussing the Pros
and Cons of Money

If you haven't guessed by now, our topic for today is money. Before we take a look at what Jesus had to say about it—and He said a lot—I'd like *you* to say something about it.

Give everyone a copy of Resource 14, "On the Money." Instruct people to answer only question 1 for now. They are to "coin" a new expression about money. Those who don't feel creative can quote an expression they've heard. Ask a few volunteers to share their expressions.

Then use your chalkboard or newsprint for the following list-making activity.

Let's make a list of what's good about money, and what's bad about it. (Some "good" possibilities: Buys necessities; easier to carry than grain or seashells; pays for things we enjoy; can be used to spread the Gospel or further God's work on earth by building church buildings and hospitals. Some "bad" possibilities: People always want more; can corrupt people; can be used on things we don't really need; makes people less reliant on God.)

On the whole, would you say money is more good than bad, or more bad than good? (Let people speculate. Jesus knew the power money can have over us, so He had a lot more negative than positive things to say about it.)

Have a volunteer read Matthew 6:24.

What makes this a tough teaching? (Many people would like to be able to serve God and money. They might pay lip service to God, but their lifestyles and choices indicate that they are actually serving money.) Point out that some versions of the Bible render the word money as "mammon." Jesus sometimes used that word to denote wealth or profit, especially that which has been gained in some unjust or unworthy way.

In what ways do people serve money? Encourage group members to share specific examples of workaholism, spending too much time maintaining possessions, making career moves solely on the basis of income, etc.

If people can "serve" money, then money can be a type of god—an object of idol worship. There's a lot of truth to the saying that whatever we think we own really owns us.

What should our attitude be about money? Jesus delivered several tough teachings on that subject. Let's come face-to-face with them.

3
Money Matters
(25-30 minutes)

Exploring What Jesus Had
to Say about Money

Call the group's attention to question 2 on Resource 14.

It would take far longer than one session to study all the things Jesus said about money. But this handout groups some of the sayings into sets. Instead of looking at each passage in detail, we'll try to glean principles for dealing with money and apply them to our situations.

To save time, form study teams and assign each set of verses to a team. Teams can then report results to the whole group. List principles on the board or newsprint.

Here are some principles, comments, and follow-up questions to help you guide the discussion.

2a. Matthew 17:24-27; Matthew 22:15-22; Luke 10:33-35
Principles:
Money is necessary; God provides it when needed.
Comments:
Regarding Matthew 17:24-27, the temple tax was an annual tax that Jewish males over 20 years of age were required to pay. It was used for upkeep of the temple. The incident shows that Jesus felt no theological obligation to pay the tax, but agreed to do so anyway.

The Matthew 22 passage also suggests that Jesus recognized that money was a necessary commodity. *The New Bible Commentary: Revised* (InterVarsity Press) **has this to say about Jesus' reply: "This was a brilliant answer, getting to the heart of the problem. Caesar represented the legal government and in that sense owned the coinage and therefore had a right to taxes. But man bears the image and likeness of God (Genesis 1:26) and**

therefore the whole of his life has a higher loyalty to the divine will."

In Luke 10:33-35, Jesus talks about the Good Samaritan using money to help the injured man. Money is part of life. It's necessary. It can be used for good.

Questions:

Do the first two passages give you any insight into your own attitude toward paying taxes?

What percentage of your income would you say is spent on necessities? What percent should be?

2b. Matthew 19:16-26

Principles:

Money is both powerful and dangerous; money is hard to give up; money can keep us from God.

Comments:

The story of the rich young ruler shows the strong hold money can have on us. The thought of a camel (the largest known animal of that region) going through the eye of a needle (probably the smallest opening His hearers could imagine) demonstrates the difficulty of entering God's kingdom when riches distract us.

Questions:

Does Jesus expect the same from us (i.e., sell everything and give it to the poor), or was this only an isolated incident?

What's the connection between giving money and eternal life? Note that we do not "buy" eternal life; it is a free gift by grace through faith in Christ. But it is necessary for us to "let go" of whatever keeps us from God in order to experience eternal life. Often the "sticking point" is money. F. F. Bruce says, "People show whether they trust in riches or not by their readiness to part with them."

2c. Matthew 6:19-24; Luke 6:24, 25; Luke 12:13-21, 31-34

Principles:

Money is temporary; money and God are mutually exclusive; money never fully satisfies.

Comments:

Money is temporary—here today and gone tomorrow. Luke 12:15 wouldn't sit too well with the person who has a bumper sticker on his new BMW that reads, "The one with the most toys at the end wins." Another bumper sticker comes much closer to the truth: "The one with the most toys at the end wins—nothing!"

Questions:

How can you tell where a person's treasure is?

What does it mean to be "rich toward God" (Luke 12:21)?

2d. Matthew 6:1-4; Luke 6:30, 31

Principles:

Money is to give; it is to be given in secret; don't expect anything in return.

Comments:

Matthew 6:1 says that giving money can be an act of righteousness, if it's done with pure motives. Luke 6:30 is one statement we might read and skip over without really thinking about how radical Jesus' words are. The context of the verse is showing love for enemies.

Questions:

What are some improper motives people might have for giving money?

Do you think most people really practice Luke 6:30? Why or why not?

2e. Mark 12:41-44; Mark 14:1-9

Principles:

The value of money is relative (a little or a lot can have the same effect); money is to be given sacrificially.

Comments:

In these passages we have two excellent examples of what it means to be "rich toward God." Both involve sacrificial giving. The widow gave virtually everything she had. The woman with the perfume gave up over a year's worth of wages to anoint Jesus. Jesus isn't saying that we shouldn't give to the poor, but that the opportunity to give to Him in person was fleeting.

Questions:

What sacrifices did each of these women make?

Can you identify with "some of those present" in Luke 14 who protested the woman's "waste" of money? If so, how?

2f. Matthew 23:16, 17, 23, 24

Principles:

Money isn't as important as we think; God cares more about our hearts than He does about our wallets.

Comments:

In verses 16 through 18 Jesus is rebuking the Pharisees for making gold and gifts in the temple and on the altar more important than the Person the temple and altar were designed to honor. In verses 23 and 24, Jesus challenges the Pharisees' motives for giving. The Pharisees thought giving 10% was enough, but God demands more—our very lives, as evidenced by our attitudes and practices in the areas of justice, mercy, and faithfulness.

Questions:

How can our money be used for justice, mercy, and faithfulness?

What do you suppose was Jesus' attitude toward tithing?

How do you think most Christians today feel about tithing?

Wrap up the Bible study, by having people recap Jesus' teaching on money in one or two sentences. Here's one possibility: "It's okay to have money, so long as you're rich toward God. It's all His anyway."

4
Now What?
(10 minutes)

Working to Develop Healthier
Attitudes toward Money

Challenge people to complete part 3 on Resource 14.

Put a star by those principles you most need to keep in mind in your daily life. **You may even want to have people come up and put stars by the principles listed on the board or newsprint without making any comment. This will provide a graphic depiction of the issues your group is dealing with.**

List some specific things you can do to have a more biblical attitude toward money. **Give people ample time to think about this one. Talk as time allows in small groups, or together in one group. Be ready to share an experience that taught you a lesson about handling money in a Christlike way, and encourage group members to do the same.**

To summarize, you may want to share the following guidelines for making a money-related decision.

Ask yourself these questions:

1. Could this inhibit me from relying on God?

2. Is it possible for this to have some power over me?

3. Might this prevent me from being "rich toward God"?

Close in prayer, bringing newly made commitments about attitudes toward money to the Lord.

If you want to prepare people for next time, pass out copies of Resource 15, "Fire and Brimstone." Encourage group members to look up the verses and answer the questions in preparation for next week's session.

5
Tough Stuff (optional)
(5-10 minutes)

Exploring the Stickier Issues

As an optional group project, ask volunteers to research the Bible's view on some of the following topics. Researchers could report their findings to the rest of the group at your next meeting.

The Bible may be silent on some of these issues, so researchers might need to seek out guiding principles to come to a conclusion.

1. Should Christians use credit cards?

2. Should Christians take out life insurance policies?

3. Should Christians store up large sums of money in savings accounts?

4. Should Christians play the stock market?

5. Should Christians buy lottery or raffle tickets?

6. Should Christians give money to ministry organizations in order to get a premium in return?

7. Are Christians expected to tithe? If so, should it be based on pre-tax or after-tax income?

FOR THE LOVE OF MONEY

1. On the back of this sheet, draw a rectangle the size of a dollar bill. (Or, if you prefer, make it the size of a hundred-dollar bill.) Scoring (you be the judge):
     a. On the money=2 points
     b. Fairly close=1 point
     c. Way off the mark=0 points

2. How long does the average U.S. dollar bill stay in circulation? (1 point)
     a. 6 months
     b. 18 months
     c. 3 years
     d. 6 years

3. How many pennies were produced in 1989 (Not counting children named Penny)? (1 point)
     a. 600,000
     b. 1.6 million
     c. 8.6 billion
     d. 16 trillion

4. Who sang the song "Money for Nothing"? (1 point)
     a. Johnny Cash
     b. Little Richard
     c. The Beatles
     d. Dire Straits

5. Approximately how much do a million dollar bills weigh? (1 point)
     a. 100 pounds
     b. 200 pounds
     c. 1 ton
     d. 2 tons

6. Who said, "Money is the root of all evil"? (1 point)
     a. Jesus
     b. The apostle Paul
     c. Mark Twain
     d. None of the above

7. Match each U.S. bill to the name of the person who is pictured on it: (1 point each)

1. $1	a. Chase
2. $2	b. Cleveland
3. $5	c. Franklin
4. $10	d. Grant
5. $20	e. Hamilton
6. $50	f. Jackson
7. $100	g. Jefferson
8. $500	h. Lincoln
9. $1,000	i. McKinley
10. $5,000	j. Madison
11. $10,000	k. Washington
12. $100,000	l. Wilson

8. Name a movie with the word "money" in the title: _____ (1 point)

ON THE MONEY

1. Coin a new expression about money:

2. Read each set of Jesus' words about money and summarize them by naming some principles for how we should view money. (Verses in parentheses are other Gospel accounts of the same teaching.)

PRINCIPLES:

a.   Matthew 17:24-27
        Matthew 22:15-22
        (Mark 12:13-17; Luke 20:20-26)
        Luke 10:33-35

b.   Matthew 19:16-26
        (Mark 10:17-27; Luke 18:18-27)

c.   Matthew 6:19-24
        Luke 6:24, 25
        Luke 12:13-21, 31-34

d.   Matthew 6:1-4
        Luke 6:30, 31

e.   Mark 12:41-44
        (Luke 21:1-4)
        Mark 14:1-9

f.   Matthew 23:16, 17, 23, 24
        (Luke 11:42)

3. Put a star by those principles you most need to keep in mind in your daily life. List some specific things you can do to have a better attitude toward money:

4. Other things Jesus said about money that you might want to look up sometime:
Luke 11:41; 14:13, 14; 16:1-15, 19-31; 19:1-27.

Fire and Brimstone

To get ready for the next session, please read Matthew 25:31-46.

Observe

(include the verses before and after the passage)

Who is this spoken to?

Where does this take place?

When does this take place?

Key words:

Contrasts:

Interpret

What is Jesus saying? (put it in your own words)

Why do you suppose Jesus said this?

List any questions this passage raises in your mind:

Apply

What is this passage saying to you personally?

What are you going to do about it?

For "extra credit": Read
Matthew 8:10-12; 13:37-43, 47-50; 22:11-14; 24:48-51; 25:28-30
Matthew 5:21, 22, 29, 30; 18:7-9; 12:33-37
Matthew 7:18-23; 25:31-46
Matthew 10:11-15; 11:20-24

FIRE AND BRIMSTONE
Is Jesus Gentle or Judgmental?

"**D**epart from me, you who are cursed, into the eternal fire prepared for the devil and his angels" (Matthew 25:41).

Many people find it hard to envision Jesus saying something like that. It sounds so harsh—because it is!

Jesus had a lot to say on the subject of hell, punishment, and judgment. In fact, there are at least 25 separate teachings on the subject in Matthew's Gospel alone. Of all the tough teachings covered in this course, this topic may be the most overlooked. We prefer to focus on God's love, not His justice; on His forgiveness, not His uncompromising holiness.

Since Jesus said so much about hell and judgment, you'll need to narrow your focus. Instead of dwelling on the details of how and when judgment will take place, you'll concentrate on steps people can take now to avoid punishment.

This rather sobering session should end on a positive note—for through Jesus Christ, God has provided an escape from condemnation.

Where You're Headed:
To examine some of Jesus' teachings about hell and judgment in order to make plans to avoid these things—and to help others avoid them.

Scriptures You'll Apply:
Matthew 25:28-46 and other Matthew passages

Things You'll Need:
- Copies of "Here Comes the Judge" (Resource 16)
- Pencils or pens
- Bibles
- Copies of "Judge for Yourself" (Resource 17)
- Chalkboard and chalk or newsprint and markers
- Copies of Resource 18, "Perfectly Holy" (optional)

1
It's a Paradox

(5 minutes)

Coming to Grips with God's
Love and His Justice

Write the following word pairs on slips of paper before the session:
- Good and evil
- First and last
- Rich and poor
- Joy and suffering
- Living and dying
- Giving and receiving
- Love and justice

When the session begins, have two people come forward and let them look at one of the slips. They should act out their pair of words, charades-style, with one taking one role and the other the opposite. Set a time limit in which the rest of the group is to guess the pair of words.

After the first pair, say: **These things are apparent opposites, but can occupy the same space, time, or person. What is that kind of pairing called?** (A paradox.)

Have volunteers act out as many of the pairs as you have time for, briefly discussing each paradox before moving on to the next. Ask: **In what ways is this a paradox?** Save "love and justice" for last and use it to introduce the day's topic.

The dictionary defines a paradox as a statement that is seemingly contradictory or opposed to common sense, but may be true. What are some paradoxes of the Christian life? (A few possibilities: People are good and evil; the first shall be last; the poor in spirit are rich; there's joy in suffering; one must die to live; to lead one must serve.)

Even God's very nature is a paradox. He's a loving Father and an uncompromising Judge. The judgmental side of God's character is the focus of our session today.

Have a volunteer read Matthew 25:41.

Is it hard or easy to imagine Jesus saying something like that? Why or why not?

For most, it's easier and more comfortable to dwell on the compassionate, loving side of God's character. Ask people to point out specific things about this verse that they have difficulty with. They might say they are bothered by the thought that God could sentence people He has created to eternal punishment in a place prepared for the devil, or that there is real suffering in the afterlife. When it comes right down to it, we all "deserve" punishment; some people may fear that they will be punished.

How could a loving God sentence people to burn in hell forever?

This is a very tough question. Instead of trying to answer it completely, discuss it long enough to get people interested in learning more about what Jesus had to say about hell and judgment.

When appropriate, you may want to explain that much of our problem with God's judgmental side may stem from our own view of fairness. We tend to assume that people are basically good and deserve good things. We tend to water down our own sinfulness, too. But we are all sinners. God seeks to bring people to Himself and doesn't wish that any should perish. Yet people continually choose to reject Him, and the inevitable consequence is separation from Him. God will not force people to accept Him.

2
A Real Downer
(5-10 minutes)

Comparing Our Views about Hell and Judgment with Biblical Descriptions

What do you think of when you hear the word "hell"?
Make a list of replies on the board or newsprint. (Some possibilities: fire, darkness, separation from God, Satan, eternal punishment, fear, loneliness, isolation, a swear word.)

If you wish, give group members some of the following background on the concept of hell from the Old and New Testaments.

There are three words for "hell" in the Bible:

1. *Sheol.* This is an Old Testament word that means "grave, hell, or pit." References include Psalm 86:13; Job 10:22, and Psalm 94:17. In the Old Testament, Sheol is sometimes used merely for "the grave" (Genesis 37:35; I Samuel 2:6) and other times appears as the opposite of the heavens (Psalm 139:8). There are some indications that those who put their trust in the Lord can escape Sheol and live in His presence (Psalm 16:9-11; 49:15; 73:24).

2. *Hades.* This is the New Testament (Greek) equivalent of Sheol. It is most often translated "hell," or "depths." References include Matthew 11:23; 16:18; Luke 10:15; 16:23. Hades was thought of as the place of departed spirits. It is a place where souls await final judgment.

3. *Gehenna.* This is the final destiny of the wicked. This is the image we most often bring to mind when thinking of hell. The word actually refers to a place outside Jerusalem that served as the city dump and incinerator. Before it became the city dump, people had sacrificed children to the god Molech there. Gehenna is a place of unquenchable fire and utter darkness, a place of weeping and gnashing of teeth. It is a place prepared by God for the devil and his angels. The references to Gehenna are the ones you'll focus on in this session.

What do you think of when you hear the word "judgment"?
List replies on the board or newsprint. (Some possibilities: sheep and goats, end times, punishment, being sentenced, guilty, courtroom, sweaty palms.)

Here's some background on judgment that you might want to share.

1. "The Bible is concerned with the fact of judgment, not with a timetable" (*New Bible Dictionary,* InterVarsity Christian Fellowship).

2. The Bible presents both God (Hebrews 12:23) and Christ (II Timothy 4:8) as the judge.

3. Judgment individual and corporate; people and nations will be judged.

4. It's past, present, and future. The world has already been judged, but the penalty hasn't been enforced yet. We stand in judgment daily due to our sinfulness.

5. The day of judgment will be a day of surprises. Some who think they deserve eternal life with God will be denied it.

6. The final basis for judgment is our relation to Christ, as evidenced by our actions.

3
Strong Words
(25-30 minutes)

Seeing How to Avoid
Hell and Judgment

Give everyone a copy of Resource 16, "Here Comes the Judge." Form four groups to look up the four sets of verses and complete their portions of the sheet. Group members should look at the verses immediately surrounding each passage to get a sense of what prompted Jesus' words.

Here are some thoughts and additional questions to guide your discussion as needed.

Group 1
Weeping and Gnashing
Matthew 8:10-12 (The Roman centurion)
Descriptions of punishment and judgment: Nation of descent doesn't matter—even subjects of the kingdom will be punished. We won't escape judgment just because we were born into a "Christian" family. The passage also suggests that people of all nations will be at the great feast.

Ways to avoid: The key to avoiding punishment is faith in Christ, which the Roman centurion demonstrated. This is the essential first step.

What specifically does it mean to "put your faith in Christ"?
Matthew 13:37-43 (Parable of the weeds)
Descriptions of punishment and judgment: Judgment will be like a harvest—a separation. Angels will do the work of separation. It's not up to us to decide who is good and who is evil; that's the Lord's work. We also learn that hell will be like a fiery furnace.

Ways to avoid: Don't cause someone to sin. Don't do evil. Be a son of the king. Be righteous. Listen to Jesus' words.

What are some ways in which we might cause sin? (See verse 41.)

Matthew 13:47-50 (Parable of the net)
Descriptions of punishment and judgment: There will be a separation of good from bad, righteous from wicked. Again we see the angels doing the work of separation. The bad are "thrown away." Hell is again referred to as a fiery furnace.

Ways to avoid: Don't be wicked; be righteous.
What is the basis of our righteousness? (See Romans 3:9-26)
Matthew 22:11-14 (Parable of the wedding banquet)
Descriptions of punishment and judgment: Many commentators suggest that the king would have provided the wedding clothes to these guests (as was the custom of the day) and this man simply failed to put his on, thereby insulting his host. The symbolic reference is to "putting on the righteousness of Christ," something else that God graciously provides to all people—but not all accept. The man failed to do something he was supposed to do and was sent to where there is weeping and gnashing of teeth. We also learn that this place is outside, utterly dark, and away from the king's presence.

Ways to avoid: Accept the King's invitation. Put on our wedding clothes (the righteousness of Christ).

How do we put on our wedding clothes, or know we have them on?

Group 2
Extreme Statements
Matthew 5:21, 22 (Anger and judgment)
Descriptions of punishment and judgment: We will be judged based on what we think as well as what we do—our attitudes as well as our actions.

Ways to avoid: Deal with your anger; don't let it go unresolved. Don't insult others.

What do you think Jesus would say about today's "insult humor" that uses put-downs and sarcasm to get laughs?

Matthew 5:29, 30; 18:7-9 (Cutting off an offending hand)
Descriptions of punishment and judgment: We will be judged by what we see (eye), what we do (hand), and where we go (foot).

Ways to avoid: Remove things that tempt us, or would cause us to sin.

What might be the equivalent of plucking out an eye or cutting off a hand or foot in today's society?

Matthew 12:33-37 (Give account of every careless word spoken)
Descriptions of punishment and judgment: We will also be judged based on what we say. Our words will either condemn us or lead to our acquittal.

Ways to avoid: Don't use careless words.

What do you suppose Jesus meant by "careless words"?
How can our words condemn us? Acquit us?

Group 3
In or Out?
Matthew 7:18-23 (The lost who say, "Lord, Lord")
Descriptions of punishment and judgment: It's an either/or proposition—either you're allowed to enter the kingdom, or you're not. Some who think they should be let in will be turned away.

Ways to avoid: Do the will of the Father. Bear good fruit. Get to know Jesus, and make sure He knows you, too.

How is it possible that someone could perform miracles, drive out demons, and prophesy in Jesus' name and still not enter the kingdom of heaven?
How do these verses make you feel?

Matthew 25:31-46 (Sheep and goats)
Descriptions of punishment and judgment: People from all nations will be judged. Either you're a sheep or a goat. Both the punishment and the reward are eternal.

Ways to avoid: Show your faith by feeding the hungry, giving drink to the thirsty, inviting strangers in, clothing the naked, caring for the sick, visiting those in prison.

If someone used these verses to build a case for salvation by works, how would you respond? (It's clear from the whole of Scripture that salvation is by grace through faith in Christ. It is also clear that those who are in Christ will bear fruit [works] that demonstrate their relationship to Christ. Both faith without works, and works without faith are "dead.")

Group 4
City Woes
Matthew 10:11-15 (Jesus' instructions to the disciples)
Descriptions of punishment and judgment: It would seem that an entire town can be judged, like Sodom and Gomorrah.
   Ways to avoid: Welcome those who are followers of Jesus.
Matthew 11:20-24 (Woe to you)
Descriptions of punishment and judgment: Again we see entire towns being judged, this time for not believing in Christ because of the miracles He performed there, and for not repenting as a result.
   Ways to avoid: Repent; believe in Christ.
   Isn't it unfair that God would judge a whole town? What about the "innocent" people? (God judges corporately and individually. He will provide a way of escape for those who remain faithful to Him. A good example of this is the story of God's protection of Lot before the destruction of Sodom in Genesis 19:1-22.)
   To summarize these many verses, ask:
   Which of these passages do you think will stick with you the most? Why?

4
Cases in Point

(5-10 minutes)

Integrating the Reality
of Judgment with Our
Everyday Lives

In order to move your discussion into more specific application to daily life, give everyone a copy of "Judge for Yourself" (Resource 17). Have group members read the short cases and discuss how they could respond.
   How could you respond to Ann? (She needs to be challenged with the words of Jesus. How do we know He was merely speaking figuratively? Even taken figuratively, wouldn't Jesus' descriptions of hell hint at some kind of separation and punishment? Is her view based on a careful examination of Scripture, or wishful thinking? Has Ann confronted her own sinfulness?)
   What can you say to Robin? (She needs to experience God's unconditional love and acceptance. Simply quoting her a string of Bible verses probably won't do the trick. She will need to confront her past in order to find healing. She should be encouraged to be part of a group where she can share openly and learn about God's love. She might also be receptive to some professional help to deal with her past.)
   How could you respond to Brett? (You could ask him where he got the idea of the "scale." Would he be interested in knowing what Jesus had to say about the subject? You might need to find out whether Brett senses any need for God in his life, and share what God means in yours.)
   What difference do Jesus' teachings on hell and judgment make in *your* life?
   What specific actions, if any, will you take in response to the passages you studied today?

Let people respond if they're willing. As needed, add comments like these:

Some in this group may not be prepared to face judgment; you can start a relationship with Christ today. Some may be overly concerned or consumed with fear about hell; you need to experience God's peace in knowing that through Jesus Christ, you can face the life to come. Some may deny the reality of eternal punishment; you may need to study Christ's words in more depth. Some may not think much about the futures of other people; you may need to share the Good News with them so they can find eternal life in Christ.

5
A Way Out
(5 minutes)

Thanking God for Providing
Jesus Christ to Lead Us
into Eternal Life

If time allows, close with a brief time of worship, thanking God for providing us with a way out of eternal punishment. Lead people into a time of prayer by reading these verses:
Psalm 16:9-11
Psalm 49:1-15, with emphasis on verse 15
Psalm 73:23-28
If you want to prepare students for next time, distribute Resource 18 ("Perfectly Holy") before they leave. Point out that next week will be your last session. Encourage group members to look up the verses and answer the questions in preparation.

6
Tough Stuff
(optional)
(5-10 minutes)

Exploring the Stickier Issues

Some evangelism approaches emphasize fear of punishment—fear of hell. Do you think they work? Do you think they should be used?
Discuss the problems of trying to "scare" people into God's kingdom. How can references to hellfire and brimstone be balanced with those that refer to God's love and compassion? Point out that Jesus didn't mince words or apologize for the reality of hell and damnation. Can evangelism approaches that minimize sin or its consequences be equally dangerous?

What about those who don't get an opportunity to hear about the claims of Christ (i.e., "the heathen")? Will God punish them eternally?
The common answer to this question is that we can't know the mind of God and must trust Him to be just—and that we should be more concerned about our own destiny because we can influence that. Is that answer sufficient, or a cop-out?

What about someone who lives a good, morally upstanding life, but doesn't enter a personal relationship with Christ? How will this person be judged?

Why must punishment be eternal? Why couldn't God have given it a shorter duration?

According to many surveys, one-third of the U.S. population describes itself as "born-again Christian." Do you believe this? Do you think some of these people might be surprised on Judgment Day?

HERE COMES THE JUDGE

Jot a few words in each column after looking up the Scripture verses.

	Descriptions of Punishment and Judgment	Ways to Avoid
Group 1 *Weeping and Gnashing* Matthew 8:10-12 Matthew 13:37-43 Matthew 13:47-50 Matthew 22: 11-14		
Group 2 *Extreme Statements* Matthew 5:21, 22 Matthew 5:29, 30; 18:7-9 Matthew 12:33-37		
Group 3 *In or Out?* Matthew 7:18-23 Matthew 25:31-46		
Group 4 *City Woes* Matthew 10:11-15 Matthew 11:20-24		

Some other verses on hell and judgment: Matthew 7:13; 10:28; 12:39-42; 19:28-30; 23:15, 33-36; Mark 12:40; Luke 12:49; 16:19-31; John 3:16-21; 5:22, 24-30; 12:30-33, 47-50; 16:8-11.

Ann is very active in her church. She says that God is love; He doesn't want any of His children to perish. He'd never sentence anyone to hell, she says. References to hell in the Bible are merely symbolic. Ultimately, all people will be saved through Christ. Ann asks you what you think. How do you respond?

Robin lives in fear of judgment every day. As a child, she had a steady diet of "fire and brimstone" sermons at church. Her parents were strictly religious and today Robin bears the scars of a dysfunctional upbringing. She "walked the aisle" when she was younger because of her desire to escape hell (and to please her parents). She's obviously a very troubled woman. What can you say to her?

Brett believes in God. He even went to Sunday school when he was younger. Today he's living his own life and doesn't think about God that much. Things like hell and judgment are the furthest things from his mind. One day in a casual conversation, Brett tells you that he figures that when his number's up, God will put all his good deeds on one side of the scale, and all his bad deeds on the other side. If the good outweighs the bad, he's in. How do you respond to him?

PERFECTLY HOLY

To prepare for next time, please read Matthew 5:21-48, focusing on verse 48.

Observe _____ *(include the verses before and after the passage)*

Who is this spoken to?

Where does this take place?

When does this take place?

Key words:

Contrasts:

Interpret _____

What is Jesus saying? *(put it in your own words)*

Why do you suppose Jesus said this?

List any questions this passage raises in your mind:

Apply_____

What is this passage saying to you personally?

What are you going to do about it?

For "extra credit": Read
Matthew 6:2, 5, 16; 7:5; 15:3-11; 23:13-32; Mark 7:6;
Luke 12:56; 13:15.

PERFECTLY HOLY
Didn't He Set the Goal Too High?

"**B**e perfect, therefore, as your heavenly Father is perfect" (Matthew 5:48).
Jesus gives us a pretty high mark to aim at. He wants us to be perfect!

With this session we come full circle. We started the course by looking at what it means to follow Jesus. Now we wrap up with where following Him is supposed to lead: to perfection. It's a tough teaching indeed, for we continually miss the mark. This session will help your group members come to grips with why Jesus said this, and what He meant by it.

As you study the Scriptures for this session, you'll find that the concept of perfection is closely linked to that of holiness. You'll also examine what Jesus had to say about hypocrisy, since it stands in stark contrast to perfect holiness.

Since we all fall short of the ideal, will you come away from this study feeling defeated? You don't have to! Using this session, let God's Word give you the strong assurance that there's hope for the hypocrite in all of us.

Where You're Headed:
To look at our own lives in light of Jesus' words in order to see how we can become more perfect in our holiness.

Scriptures You'll Apply:
Matthew 5:21-48 and other Gospel passages

Things You'll Need:
• Copies of "Perfection Detection" (Resource 19)
• Pencils or pens
• Three or more pennies and a cup (optional)
• Bibles
• Concordances, Bible dictionaries, and commentaries (optional)
• Copies of "Holy Hypocrites!" (Resource 20)
• Chalkboard and chalk or newsprint and markers

1
Be Perfect

(5-10 minutes)

Demonstrating How
Hard It Is to Be Perfect

As people arrive, give them copies of "Perfection Detection" (Resource 19). Tell them you're trying to find someone who's perfect, and this handout will weed out those who are imperfect.

1. The first instruction asks people to draw a perfect circle with their eyes closed. Have participants critique each other's work. Choose the one that is closest to perfect, and then decide whether it really is perfect.

2. For the second instruction, have people put down their pencils and pens and listen as you read the following 15-digit number: 123409173928603. After you read it, they are to write it down perfectly from memory. See who can remember it completely (probably no one will).

3. See whether anyone can do this pencil-or-pen-balancing for 60 seconds. Have people write down their scores. They get only one try at this balancing act.

4. See whether anyone comes up with something he or she can do perfectly.

5. Is it possible to be perfect? This question is your lead-in to the session. Let people share their written answers. Rather than trying to reach consensus, simply use the question to arouse curiosity. Give group members a moment to mark their Perfect-o-Meters; then move on with an introduction like the following.

Is there any parallel between this exercise and the Christian life? (Some possibilities: We always fall short of the mark; it's not easy; we may use strange measurements to tell whether we're perfect.)

In Matthew 5:48 Jesus tells His followers to "Be perfect." Today we're going to explore this verse in depth and try to figure out what He meant by it.

2
The Pursuit
of
Perfection

(10-15 minutes)

Better Understanding Jesus'
Command to Be Perfect

Form at least two teams. Give each team the same assignment—to answer this question: **What did Jesus mean by saying, "Be perfect" in Matthew 5:48?**

Let teams meet for five to ten minutes and see what they come up with. Encourage them to look at the verse in context, and look up other verses that might be cross-referenced.

Tell participants that the words *therefore* and *as* are key. "Therefore" suggests we need to look at what Jesus was talking about prior to saying this. "As" suggests we need to determine what it means to say that God is perfect. If you wish, have Bible dictionaries, commentaries, and concordances on hand. But use them only after teams have struggled with their own interpretations of the verse, using just their Bibles.

Have teams report their findings. Here are some things you could add if the groups don't cover them:

1. The immediate context of the verse is after Jesus tells people to love their enemies. This suggests that Jesus is telling His followers to have perfect love, just as God has perfect love. His love is unconditional—He loves the just and the unjust, the righteous and the unrighteous. We should do the same. Jesus may also be talking

about perfect fairness, as God is unbiased in His dealings with all people (see vss. 45, 46).

2. The larger context of the verse is the Sermon on the Mount. Jesus uses these words after presenting six "You have heard that it was said . . . but I say . . ." statements, giving stricter interpretations of the law than even the Pharisees were accustomed to. Keeping the law isn't enough; true obedience involves our hearts, motives, and attitudes. This implies that being perfect is more than following a set of rules.

3. Many Bibles cross-reference this verse with Leviticus 19:2—"Be holy, because I, the Lord your God, am holy." This suggests a connection between perfection and holiness.

4. Jesus uses the word "perfect" in one other place. In Matthew 19:21 He tells the rich young ruler that to be perfect, the man should sell all his possessions, give to the poor, and follow Jesus. Again, following the laws isn't enough.

Have teams report other findings. Then continue the discussion with questions like the following:

Does Jesus expect us to be perfect? Or do you think He expects us to fall short, but merely aim at being perfect?

There is disagreement among Bible scholars about this. You might emphasize that Jesus wants us to continue moving closer to perfection. He provides the supreme example of living a perfect life. Everyone else has sinned, so none of us is perfect. But the Holy Spirit can help us become more Christlike.

What's the difference between being perfect and being a perfectionist? Is Jesus calling us to be perfectionists? (Being a perfectionist [in the sense that most people use the word] pushes you to try to be perfect on your own—which is impossible. We are called to be Christlike, but can do so only by relying on the power of God's Spirit. Perfectionism sometimes leads to obsession with details that aren't really moral issues—whether the floor is vacuumed under the bed, whether the pictures on the wall are straight, etc. Christlike perfection includes Christlike priorities.)

Let's list some of the ways that God is perfect. What would it mean for us to be more perfect in those ways?

As needed, point out that God is perfect in terms of His work (Deuteronomy 32:4); His way (II Samuel 22:31; Psalm 18:30); and His law (Psalm 19:7; James 1:25). Group members might say He's perfect in terms of His love, justice, creation, mercy, morality, holiness, and in other ways.

God's moral character is perfect; He is completely holy. We'll spend the rest of the session looking at holiness and how we can be more holy. We'll talk about how to avoid the opposite, too.

3
Making the Connection

Contrasting Holiness
and Hypocrisy

What does it mean to be holy? (Some dictionary definitions: Set apart; characterized by perfection and transcendence: commanding absolute adoration and reverence; spiritually pure. When we think of God's holiness, we think of His absolute moral perfection. There isn't even a hint of a flaw in His character.)

What's the opposite of holy? (Evil, immoral, impure, sinful, blemished, etc.)

See whether anyone mentions hypocrisy or something similar. If not, get people to see that what Jesus condemned more than anything else wasn't their immorality, but their hypocrisy—pretending to be one thing when they were really something else. The dictionary defines a hypocrite as "One who feigns to be what one is not or to believe what one does not; a play actor." Most often when Jesus used the word, He was also referring to people as being "godless."

Throughout the Gospels we see examples of blatant sinners being closer to the kingdom of God than religious hypocrites were. Can you think of examples? (See the stories of the Pharisee and the publican; the woman caught in adultery; the sinful woman who anoints Jesus; Zacchaeus, etc.)

The blatant sinner is at least aware of his or her shortcomings. The hypocrite does everything possible to conceal shortcomings. In this part of the Sermon on the Mount, Jesus is attacking people's tendency to follow the letter of the law, but with impure motives. He's condemning their hypocrisy.

In order to look more closely at what Jesus had to say about hypocrisy, give everyone a copy of Resource 20, "Holy Hypocrites!" This handout looks at several instances in which Jesus condemned people for their hypocrisy. Work through the handout as a large group or in smaller groups.

Matthew 7:5 (plank in the eye)

What's the source of the hypocrisy that Jesus is condemning? (Jesus is condemning people for their blindness to their own faults—for criticizing or judging others when they have much to be criticized for themselves.)

Give an example of similar hypocrisy that might happen today. (Here's one example: One person in the church is flabbergasted that another member smokes cigarettes, when the judging person has a real weight problem.)

Luke 12:56 (interpreting the times)

What's the source of the hypocrisy that Jesus is condemning? (Blindness to God's work in the world, or in their own lives; the people's failure to respond to Jesus at this time.)

Give an example of similar hypocrisy that might happen today. (Someone who continues to put off a decision to follow Christ, even though the time is right.)

Luke 13:15 (Sabbath healing)

What's the source of the hypocrisy that Jesus is condemning? (A distorted sense of values. The synagogue ruler was not pleased that Jesus healed this crippled woman on the sabbath. Jesus directs His "You hypocrites" remark to more than one person, implying that others at the scene must have felt the same way. Jesus rebukes the people for "breaking" the sabbath in order to give an ox a drink, but not wanting to see a person healed on the sabbath.)

Give an example of similar hypocrisy that might happen today. (Members of a church are angry with the pastor for failing to show up at their anniversary celebration, even though he was engaged in a crisis counseling situation at the time.)

Matthew 15:3-11; Mark 7:6-8 (clean and unclean)

What's the source of the hypocrisy that Jesus is condemning? (Placing too much value on human traditions. The tradition Jesus attacks here was a Jewish son's devoting a certain amount of his income to God, thereby relieving himself of the responsibility to care for his aging parents with that money. This tradition is based on Numbers 30:1, 2. Often the money devoted to God was not used for sacred purposes. This was a violation of God's command to honor one's parents.)

Give an example of similar hypocrisy that might happen today. (One church member standing in the way of needed progress, saying, "We've never done it that way before.")

Matthew 23:13, 15, 23, 25, 27-32 (Woe to you!)

What's the source of the hypocrisy that Jesus is condemning? (Jesus condemns the teachers of the law for quite a few things here; they all boil down to ignorance of God's real demands. The religious leaders had set up a system of rituals to keep themselves pure, but Jesus saw that they were only clean on the outside. Inside they were full of greed and self-indulgence. They lacked compassion, justice, mercy, and faithfulness. Jesus also condemns the idea that this system of ritual purification and adherence to the law will earn the leaders favor with God though they neglect more important things.)

Give an example of similar hypocrisy that might happen today. (An office worker goes to church Sunday after Sunday, but always gets to work late and leaves early during the rest of the week.)

Matthew 6:2, 5, 16 (giving, prayer, and fasting)

What's the source of the hypocrisy that Jesus is condemning? (Love of display, doing things for show, without real righteousness. He specifically rebukes flashy giving, showy prayers, and self-serving fasting.)

Give an example of similar hypocrisy that might happen today. (A wealthy benefactor donates a large sum of money to an organization for a new building, provided the building bears his or her name.)

One word of caution, thinking back to Matthew 7:5. It's easy for us to find hypocrisy in others. At times it may seem like the "national pastime" of the church! It's more difficult to find and deal with hypocrisy in our own lives. But that's where our focus should stay.

4
Help for Hypocrites
(10 minutes)

Facing Hypocrisy
in Ourselves

To get people thinking about their own lives, have them answer the two questions at the bottom of Resource 20.

One way I have been a hypocrite lately, or know I can be a hypocrite:

Something specific I can do to be less hypocritical in this area:

Encourage sharing as people are willing, and time allows. If your group is large, people may be more comfortable sharing in a smaller group, or possibly even one-on-one.

Help group members see that we can only take steps to rid ourselves of hypocrisy if we face up to it and seek God's help to rid us of it. Only then can we move closer to the perfection Jesus wants for us.

Close in prayer, thanking God for the life and words of Jesus that we have as our example for living. Ask God to help group members keep any commitments made during this course.

5
Tough Stuff (optional)
(5-10 minutes)

Exploring the Stickier Issues

If you see someone who is obviously being hypocritical, should you confront that person, or simply pay attention to your own "planks"?

If someone said he or she didn't go to church because it's full of hypocrites, how would you respond?

Why is it that many people seem to find more love, genuineness, and acceptance at an Alcoholics Anonymous (or other support group) meeting than at church?

If time allows, briefly review highlights of the course.

What is one important thing you learned from this group that you can apply to your life?

How has your view of Jesus changed, if at all?

What do you consider Jesus' toughest teaching now that we've looked at some of them?

Many of the sessions touched on the fact that there's more to the Christian life than a one-time confession of faith. Based on that fact, do you think there are a lot of people who think they are "saved" who probably aren't?

If desired, wrap up the course with comments like these:

It's clear from the teachings of Jesus that there's no place for so-called "nominal" Christianity. Jesus calls us to total commitment, total forgiveness, true faith, freedom from money's clutches, and ultimately perfection itself. Even when we mess up, He's there to forgive and give us another try. Our job is to continue to stay close to Him in order get to know Him more fully, and then seek to live as He directs. Yes, it's tough—but it's also the best possible way to live.

PERFECTION DETECTION

Follow these instructions to determine how perfect you are. Then mark the Perfect-o-meter at the bottom of this page to indicate how perfect you think you are.

1. Draw a perfect circle with your eyes closed.

2. Put down your writing implement and listen to your leader read a number. Then pick up your writing implement and write down that number perfectly from memory (no tape recorders allowed!).

3. Balance the same writing implement perfectly still on your middle finger for as long as you can. You get only one try. A perfect score is 60 seconds. Have someone time you and write your score here: _____ seconds

4. Write down something (anything) you are perfect at.

5. Is it possible to be perfect?

Given your performance on the above exercises, and everything else you know about yourself, mark where you think you should be on the Perfect-o-Meter.

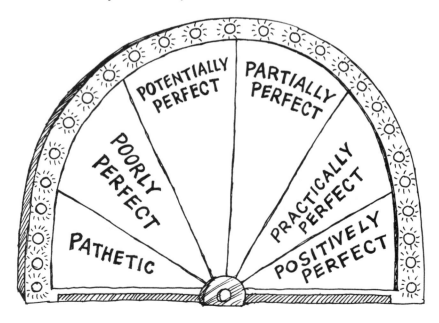

HOLY HYPOCRITES!

Matthew 7:5

What's the source of the hypocrisy that Jesus is condemning?

Give an example of similar hypocrisy that might happen today:

Luke 12:56

What's the source of the hypocrisy that Jesus is condemning?

Give an example of similar hypocrisy that might happen today:

Luke 13:15

What's the source of the hypocrisy that Jesus is condemning?

Give an example of similar hypocrisy that might happen today:

Matthew 15:3-11; Mark 7:6-8

What's the source of the hypocrisy that Jesus is condemning?

Give an example of similar hypocrisy that might happen today:

Matthew 23:13, 15, 23, 25, 27-32

What's the source of the hypocrisy that Jesus is condemning?

Give an example of similar hypocrisy that might happen today:

Matthew 6:2, 5, 16

What's the source of the hypocrisy that Jesus is condemning?

Give an example of similar hypocrisy that might happen today:

One way I have been a hypocrite lately, or know I can be a hypocrite:

Something specific I can do to be less hypocritical in this area: